New Dimensions in Healing Yourself

Rev. Hanna Kroeger
Illustrated by Alberto Kroeger

New Dimensions in Healing Yourself
by Rev. Hanna Kroeger

© 1991 by Hanna Kroeger Publications
2nd Printing 1996

ISBN 1-883713-09-9

Table of Contents

Introduction

This book is meant to give you some real confidence and practical information on healing and how you can truly help yourself and others. So many times we find ourselves going to others for the answers in regards to our problems. What a job for even the best of doctors, priests, ministers and counselors—to dig to the bottom of your trouble, to untangle the tangled, to uncover what was previously concealed, when most of the time we, in our intuitive nature, can, when pressed, disclose exactly the source or point of origin—the moment, the statement spoken, the grief experienced, the hurtful words heard—where the breakdown, now manifesting in the physical, began.

Be your own detective. The use of all others outside of yourself should be but a support system for your learning. KNOW THYSELF.

I have decided to start this book with the spiritual aspect. In my other books and writings I have started with the physical, gone to the emotional and ended with the spiritual, that so often people get caught up in the physical, as in life, and touch upon but never dig into the spiritual teachings of healing.

We are entering the Aquarian Age. Many things are changing, including the concept of healing.

For instance, we used to lay all responsibility for our healing on the physicians, the priests or the medicine man. Not any longer. We recognize that it is greatly our responsibility to stay well and to search every avenue to be healed, if needed. Included are our physicians, chiropractors, nutritionists and those that show us spiritual and mental energies which lay unused and dormant in the depth of our being.

In Chapter 30 of *Deuteronomy* it is written:

> Therefore choose life.
> It is up to us to choose, so do it now.

Only His disciples learned where to apply the hands. This book is an accumulation of a lifetime of research and will teach you how to do the job and where to place your hands.

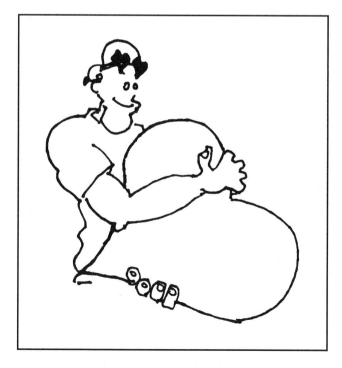

I gave a beggar from my little store
from my well earned gold.
He spent the shining ore
and came again, again and again
still hungry as before.

I gave a thought.
And with this thought of mine
he found himself
the man supreme divine.

He glows, enriched with blessings
as never yet before
and now he begs
for earthly things no more.

Author Unknown

It is important to remember that no illness ever resulted from a single cause. There are always several causes present. It stands to reason that there is not a single method of healing therapy. Best results in healing come from the combination of therapies.

I. SOUL LEVEL

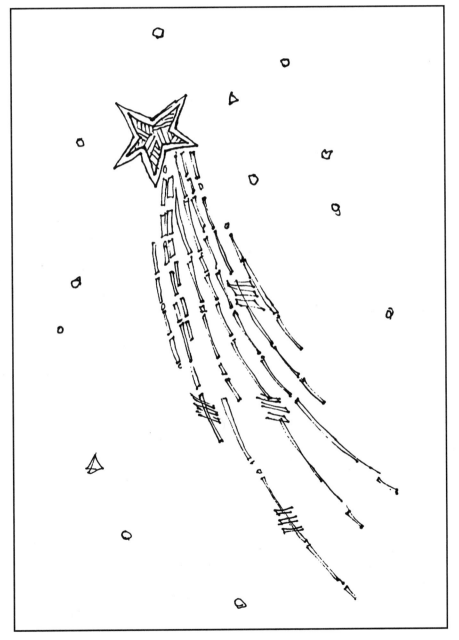

I. SOUL LEVEL

Balancing the Aura and Its Energy Centers

Synchronizing Your Brain

Grief

Jealousy

Depression

Lack of Self-Confidence

Forgiving

Sorrow

Exhaustion

Resentments

(All of these negative traits
have a direct influence on your aura
and your physical body.)

Prayer Action Plan for Dissolving
the Spiritual Cause of a Physical Problem

Prepare Yourself Spiritually for
the Most Precious Gift of God:
YOUR BABY

**Problems of the Soul Level Can Be Expressed
in the Following Physical Natures:**

- Heart trouble
- Low blood pressure
- High blood pressure
- Emotional troubles
- Paralyzed condition in parts or total
- Cramps
- Rheumatism
- Mental illnesses
- Mental limitations

Balancing the Aura
and its Energy Centers

In order to help, we have to realize the following facts. Most probably you have heard of the word *chakra*. This word is taken from the philosophy of the East and it means *energy center*.

Unfortunately, we take the teachings from the East without examination or evaluation on our part.

They teach:
1. Root-chakra
2. Bowel-chakra
3. Solar plexus-chakra
4. Heart-chakra
5. Neck-chakra
6. Third eye-chakra
7. Crown-chakra

That gives 7 chakras.

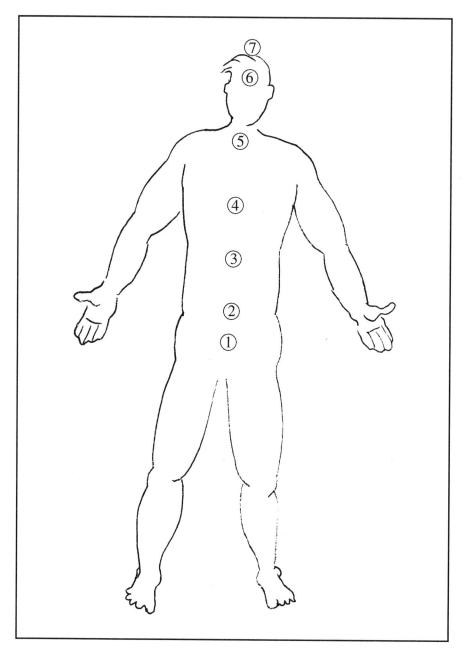

**The 7 Chakras of the Eastern Man
and the Eastern Philosophy**

The Eastern man recognizes 7 chakras which he brings into balance by:

- Lotus position (cross legged sitting)
- Mantra repetition
- Meditation
- Incense

The American Indian has 8 chakras which he brings into balance by:

- Sweat baths
- Circle dances
- Sage incense
- Drumming

The Western man has 9 chakras. His methods to bring the light centers to work are:

- Prayer
- Singing
- Action
- Visualization
- Contemplation

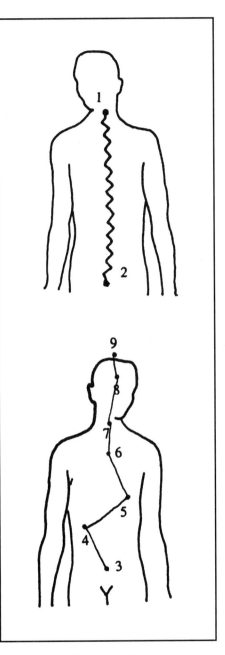

**The 9 Light Centers
of the Western Man**

The Colors of the Nine Light Centers

1. Red
2. Orange
3. Yellow
4. Green
5. Blue
6. Magenta
7. Violet
8. Pink
9. White

In order to bring these light centers into balance, we have 2 methods.

First Method

Visualize the centers with the respective colors and balance them by visualization. This takes about 10 minutes total.

Second Method

Intake and output have to be alike. So, fold your hands and make a triangle over No. 1, which is the seventh vertebra. Ask loudly for the color red, the universal power, the color of strength, for 30 seconds. Then place your hands above the head, going up and down, saying "intake and output have to be alike." Do this for 30 seconds and the miracle is that all centers are aligned, all at once.

Synchronizing Your Brain

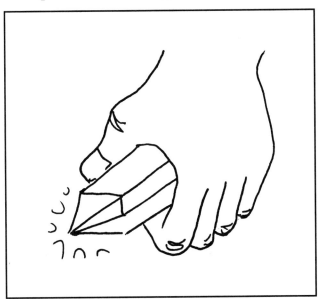

After you have balanced your light centers, synchronize your brain. Your brain is your control tower. It has to be in balance. Take a crystal in your left hand. The crystal should not be cut, one side being rough. A crystal is a tool which multiplies your thoughts many times.

Talk to the crystal: "I will that you become an instrument of our Lord, that you help to balance this person's brain."

Now take each section of the brain and say, "In the name of the Most High, be balanced!" Go from section to section, No. 5 is last. Every time ask for balance. Now you are in balance. Now you are ready to heal others. Give thanks to our Lord.

How do you know when your brain is out of balance? When one shoulder is higher than the other. When one leg is shorter than the other. When right eye droops. When jaw is misaligned.

Hold hands together. One hand will be longer. Synchronize the brain and all that comes into balance.

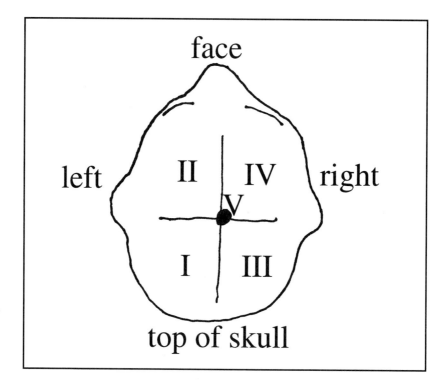

Grief

How to Deal with Grief

Whenever we lose a beloved one, naturally we grieve. However, some of us grieve so intensely that we cannot carry on with our lives. We go from physician to minister, from priest to friends, and all say the same: "You will get over the loss in time."

The person in grief is blocked in life, so is the aura of the parted one. Excessive, prolonged grief holds the aura of the parted one and he is in limbo.

You have to let go. By all means you have to let go. The following ceremony will help you.

Every day for 14 days (some of us need more time) do the following ritual. Put a mat on the floor in a way that your head will be north. Light 7 candles and place them in a wide circle around the mat. Lightly colored candles such as pink, blue or white are best. Now lie relaxed on the mat. Meditate and pray. After a while, talk to your beloved one in the following manner: "I release you, I love you. Because I love you I will not grieve any longer, so you can be happy. Go on to your new task." Talk to your parted one and stay relaxed for 30 minutes and know that all is well. Repeat if needed.

Jealousy

Jealousy is one of the most destructive emotions a person can carry. It causes all kinds of physical ailments.

- Stomach trouble
- Aches and pains
- Indigestion
- Headaches
- Lung trouble
- Liver trouble

Jealousy is like a boil which is emptying its foul content into your beautiful body.

The following method works for most people to overcome jealousy. Make a tea of:

2 oz cyany flower
2 oz chamomile
2 oz rose petal
2 oz orange blossom
2 oz spearmint

Mix. Take 1 tsp. of this mixture to 1 cup of boiling water. Drink 1 cup. Then place your middle finger of your right hand 2 inches below your bellybutton. Hold middle finger of left hand on the back of the skull. Say loudly, "I release the jealousy which I carry towards (say name or situation). I release this negative entity now and I am free from a burden which made me sick and not fully productive. Jealousy stood in my way to Christ." It is released now.

We realize that jealousy is the root of hate, war, disease, resentment and marriage trouble. It is worth fighting against this huge, destructive force. Jealousy is one big factor that holds you back from spiritual growth and spiritual advancement. It is like a magnet which draws all ills, pain and fear to you. You have to make personal and sacrificial effort to release jealousy, then all other difficulties will be solved.

Another Method

Relax in a chair. Have a glass of water next to you. Pile up all difficulty and jealousy you might have towards a person or a situation and throw it into the water. After a few minutes, throw this water down the drain. Do not give it to a plant. The plant will wither. Now fill the cup with water and add 1 tsp. apple cider vinegar. Fill the good thoughts of your inner self into the water, then drink it. All jealousy is gone and you start a new life. To release *resentment*, do the same thing.

Depression

Sometimes we suffer from depression, which we desire to overcome quickly. The following method is highly advisable. However, if your depression comes from low blood sugar syndrome, Candida albicans or any other serious physical ailment, it will not help.

You have to use a lot of energy to keep yourself depressed. You are turning your anger inside. Frequently, depression is anger turned within. If you let go, depression can be eliminated.

Hold the points as indicated in the diagram.

For Fear and Depression

Hold the same points and, in addition, the right side below the floating rib, the inside of both elbows and on the right middle finger. Fear and distrust with depression is always experienced when you do not breathe deeply and exhale fully. Put deep breathing into your program.

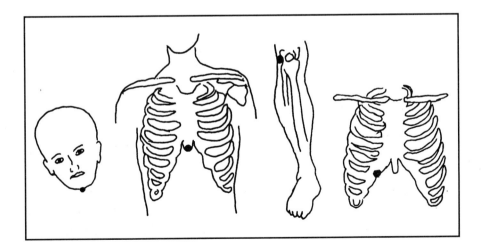

Lack of Self-Confidence

Lack of self-confidence can bring a person to highest performance or it can toss his life into total misery. In severe cases, psychotherapy is needed. However, you could try the following method which works fast and is inexpensive.

Press behind both ears. You will find a bony indentation. Hold this for 30 seconds. Next, press the points (right and left) under the skull, as shown in the picture, for 30 seconds. In addition, press firmly in the middle of your feet for 30 seconds. Lastly, press on the heel, as shown in the picture, for 30 seconds. Do this every morning and every night.

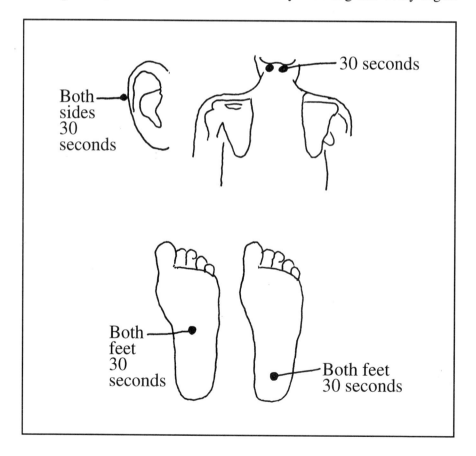

Forgiving

One of the greatest difficulties we have to overcome is forgiving—forgiving ourselves and forgiving others. Serious illnesses carry a seed of unforgiving in your mind and heart and it is like acid eating away at your health. Our Lord Jesus suffering on the cross said, "Father, forgive them." It was so important to him, forgiving, that He mentioned it in His last hour.

The following method, given to us by Dr. Duane Anderson, is a tremendous help.

Stand straight with the middle finger of your right hand touching the left back side of the scalp (No. I) and, with a rubbing motion, say, "In the name of our Lord I forgive myself and I forgive (place, name). I forgive totally."

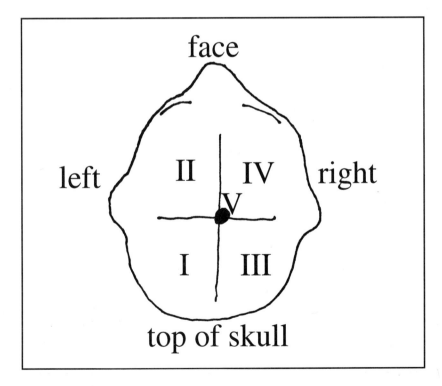

With the middle finger of the right hand, touch No. II and say the same and do the same rubbing motion. With the middle finger of the left hand on No. III, say the same. With the middle finger of left hand on No. IV, say the same again. Place your right hand above bellybutton and, in clockwise motion 7 or more times, say, "I forgive myself, I forgive those that did me wrong." *A great relief will come over you.* At the same time, rub around your navel 7 times (see picture below).

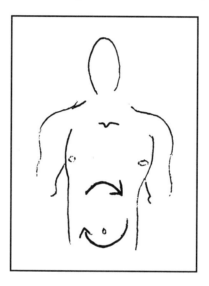

Sorrow

Hold your hands over your heart. Cup your hands and visualize placing your heart into your hands. Slowly move your cupped hands forward, visualizing giving your heart to the Lord. Then offer the heart and your sorrow, love and life to God.

For Sadness

Cross legs. With right leg over top of left leg, place left hand below knees and with right hand press on instep of right foot. Then reverse it.

Exhaustion

The seat of exhaustion is situated 4 finger widths below the navel. It is called Hara, an old Sanskrit word.

Place left hand over Hara, right hand over left hand and hold it that way. Breathe in slowly, bring breath to forehead. Exhale forcefully, holding tongue on roof of mouth. Do this breathing 6 times in a row.

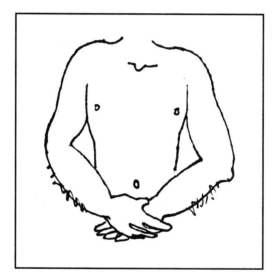

Resentments

Release Hidden Resentments

1. Firmly stroke with both hands over your face and head. Start on your chin and slowly move up to your forehead, over your hair to the back of your head and end in the neck. Start over again: chin—forehead—back of head—neck. Do this several times. It will release resentments, even childhood resentments and hidden anger.

2. In the evening write all your angers, resentments or shortcomings on a piece of paper. Not an old piece of scratch paper but a nice piece of paper, as if you would write a letter to a dear friend. Do not read it. Put it in a drawer. Next morning read it and burn it. In the evening do it again. Do this until all resentment is gone— 1 week or 3 days—it depends on you. This is cheaper than burdening a psychiatrist with your troubles. This will release pain, sore throat and even cancer.

3. Sit on a chair and press your thumbs in the middle of your thighs. Say the words:

   Ah-Kai-Ion
   Ah is the color gold,
   Kai is the color blue,
   Ion is the color white.

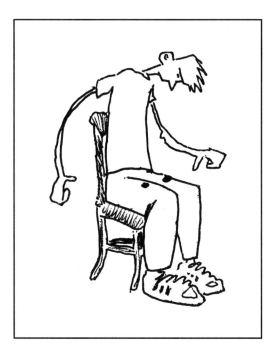

This will remove unpleasant memory patterns to which resentments are one of them.

Anger

Anger can go into hate. Hate is extremely destructive to the liver. The liver has to detoxify the chemicals, environmental poisons, metal poisons and so on. If one is in hate, the liver cannot do its job and the poison goes into the bloodstream, making all kinds of trouble such as allergies, flu, hives, mood swings and emotional upsets.

Prayer Action Plan
for Dissolving the Spiritual Cause
of a Physical Problem

The Hawaiian Kahunas used to get rid of unwanted negative attitudes and feelings by relaxing and commanding these unwanted negative attitudes to leave their bodies while they shook their right and left legs.

I suggest:

1. Review the situation that is presently causing a particular emotional stress.

2. Pick a word that expresses the positive opposite of this negative emotion (example: hate—love; anxiety—security; worry—confidence; impatience—patience, etc.).

3. Place a glass of water next to you.

4. Relax. See yourself beset with the negative emotion. Put it all into the glass of water. Throw water away.

5. Take a fresh cup, preferably porcelain. Fill this cup with water and think that this water contains the necessary solution to your problem—it is filled with the opposite positive emotion. Drink the water, knowing that you are filling yourself with the positive emotion you need, and the negativity will leave you when you next urinate.

6. End session. Then urinate, feeling an exhilaration of positivity.

Prepare Yourself Spiritually for the Most Precious Gift of God: YOUR BABY

Life Begins

With so much strife and controversy in this country concerning abortion, we thought it timely to address this issue according to our philosophy. We teach, as do other spiritual traditions, that we are inhabitants of a physical body—an immortal spirit that goes from one physical birth to another for the awakening of our true God self.

After conception, the dense physical form begins to grow within the womb. During the first 4 months, the embryo continually changes from (passing through all the evolutionary kingdoms) first mineral, then plant, fish, animal and, finally, human. After the fourth month, the embryo is called a fetus. At this time the heart seed atom from the awaiting soul passes down into the fetus. This marks the quickening, the moment when life has begun for the unborn child.

After the quickening, there is a soul involved. But since the soul does not take "ownership" of the body until physical birth, a miscarriage or abortion after the fourth month causes the awaiting soul simply to withdraw and await another opportunity for incarnation.

After the quickening, archangel Gabriel and his flock of angels prepare the soul for its task on earth. The Bible talks about how the numbered soul enters with the first breath of the child. The soul, thus prepared by Gabriel's angelic beings, now takes full possession of the entire being and it becomes a living soul, as the Bible points out.

I call the blessed children our Lord's children. They are so different. They do not give their parents trouble. They are healthy and well poised. They are loving and full of unusual ideas. When other children are destructive, they rebuild and repair. They do not want foolish things, nor do they cry and carry on as other children do. In my opinion it is the best thing one can do for their children. Bless them daily while they are still in the womb of their mother.

One of these blessed children came to my house. She was 5 years old. A lovely, quiet child. She looked around and said to me, "If you place your desk another way, you will have more room in your house." When she passed the Lord's picture, she made the sign of the cross. And all about her was so natural and balanced, so loving, quiet and intelligent. We wanted to leave the house and turn off the lights but this little girl thought of the cat and said "Don't turn off all the lights; the cat does not like the darkness."

A family of 5 children, after they heard my talk, blessed their last child. The mother reported that the girl is the healthiest of all her children.

How to Bless an Unborn Baby

I tell every young expecting mother to bless the unborn baby every day in the following fashion: Put your left hand out and your right hand over the baby in the womb but do not touch the mother's body. Now bless the unborn with your deepest feeling and prayers and talk to the heavenly creator.

When it is rebellious and kicks a lot, the father should do it. You will see the baby calm down immediately. In case the baby is in an upside-down position, turn the baby in the following manner: Someone with authority, like the father, stands on the right side of the expecting mother. He puts the opened left hand on the neck of the mother but, again, does not touch her. The right hand, put over the unborn (not touching) and say, "In the name of Jesus our Lord, I command that you turn into the right position. Turn, turn, turn." And here the baby will turn immediately and peacefully.

II. MIND LEVEL

"To think is the hardest work there is. This is most probably the reason why so few people engage in it."

—Henry Ford

II. MIND LEVEL

Healing Through Mind Power

Thought: The Architect of Destiny

Functions of Thought Power

Activate Your Sleeping Will Power

Increase Intelligence

Enthusiasm

Mental Clarity

The Development of Thought Power

Healing Through Mind Power

Congestion of the mind can express itself in the physical realm as:

- Heart trouble
- Low blood pressure
- High blood pressure
- Emotional troubles
- Paralyzed condition in parts or total
- Cramps
- Rheumatism
- Mental illnesses
- Mental limitations
- Accidents
- Bone trouble
- Leukemia
- Stiff joints
- Deafness
- Congestion in digestive tracts

Thought:
The Architect of Destiny

If the mind dwells continually upon one train of thought, a groove is formed into which the thought force runs automatically and such a habit of thought survives death. And since it belongs to the ego, it is carried over to the subsequent earth life as a thought tendency and capacity.

Thought Power Creates Environments

It is often said that man is the result of his environmental forces. This is not true. We cannot believe this because the facts always prove the contrary. Many of the world's greatest men have been born in poverty and in adverse conditions.

Many who have been born into slums and filthy surroundings have risen to the highest statuses in the world. They have won laurels of fame and distinguished themselves in politics, literature and poetry. They have become brilliant geniuses and beacon lights of the world. How do you account for this?

Functions of Thought Power

Thought and Modern Science

Thought is the greatest force on earth. Thought is the most powerful weapon in the armor of a saint. Constructive thought transforms, renews and builds. The far-reaching possibilities of this force were most accurately developed to perfection by the ancient and put to the highest possible use, for thought is the primal force at the origin of all creation; the genesis of the entire phenomenal creation is given as a single thought that arose in the cosmic mind.

However, the forces of thought, which are wireless messages, have to have an impulse. This impulse is found in the *mitro-genetic rays*. These are rays which appear for the first time in the brain. It has been found that when the frontal lobes of the brain are closer together, more of the mitro-genetic rays are released. We know that the mitro-genetic rays differ in both quality and quantity. We know that by stimulating the frontal lobes, thoughts become streamlined and powerful.

The mitro-genetic ray is *the real transporter of a thought*. Without this ray, a thought is a bird without wings. The mitro-genetic ray gives the spark needed so that thoughts become reality. Born healers all are born with a powerful mitro-genetic ray. We have to stimulate this ray. The following method is terrific to streamline and to give spark to your thoughts. Hold points indicated for 30 seconds.

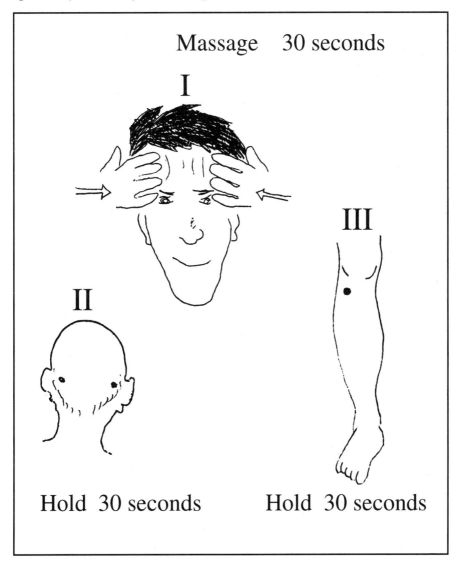

Energy Follows Thought

This is one of the laws of the universe. We have to keep this in mind when discussing *diseases*. If we have happy and constructive thoughts, energy will follow these kinds of thoughts and build a healthy body and a happy environment.

If we entertain thoughts of hate, envy, jealousy or fear, we invite dark brothers and energies of darkness. If you come in such a trend of unproductive thoughts, stand in front of your mirror and say loudly, "Stop, stop, stop!" and all the dark brothers leave and make room for angels.

It is important to remember that no illness ever resulted from a single cause. There are always several causes present. It stands to reason that there is not a single method of healing therapy. Best results in healing come from the combining of therapies.

Activate Your Sleeping Will Power

How do we develop thinking? Thinking develops if you learn how to concentrate, meditate, pray and serve your fellow man. Learning is not thinking. Learning is mechanical. It is filling your brain with data which is needed to develop the power of thoughts. Thinking is the ability to translate ideas to meet the needs of life.

An idea is an impulse, a vision, a message, and here come thinking and understanding which translate an idea to meet a need of your life or the life of someone else. Ideas are projections from higher sources. Your thoughts have to translate the ideas into something constructive.

Speaking of constructive thinking, there are two kinds. One kind of thinking is egocentric. You take an idea and translate it with your thought into disturbed behavior. History is full of these types. Ego thinkers are selfish, anti-survival and destructive. You find ego thinkers in religion, in human relationships and in politics.

Others are soul thinkers who think in constructive, progressive and healing ways. All true healers are constructive soul thinkers and here is the point I want to make: The power of thought must be translated into soul thinking. Then you can heal. You can heal your own body and that of others. People said that my father died of a massive heart attack when he was 52, so I thought I would have a heart attack also. My grandmother died of diabetes. Will I also contract that disease? My sister has cancer, so do I have that also? Where is my cancer?

My cancer, your cancer, our cancer—why not get rid of the negative patterns and change your lifestyle? Your eating habits are lousy, so why not change those and your thinking also? Your powerhouse of thoughts is in your front brain. Get after this powerhouse. It will translate the idea of health into your body and make it healthier. Say 3 times, "Dear Father, please take the life giving force of thought to flow through each cell of my being." Now every cell is healed, every cell is regenerated.

> **Thought regenerates and heals on the cellular level.**

Increase Intelligence

Press thumbs on both temples and at the same time take a deep, slow breath. Then press thumb of left hand on middle of forehead above and between the eyes and press thumb of right hand on outside corner of right eye. Take another deep breath, hold mouth tight and puff out cheeks.

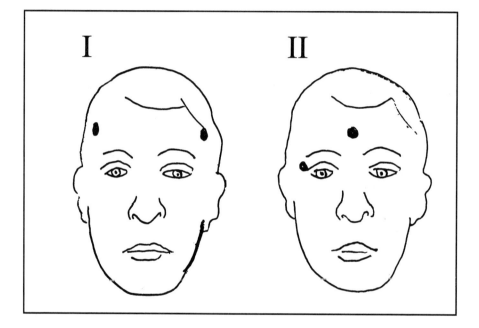

Enthusiasm

Enthusiasm is electrifying. It is an inward fire. It is God's finger. It is God's divine breath.

A powerful belief is carried by powerful and enthusiastic personalities. Enthusiastic and daring people are quiet about their future dreams. They are steadfast. "The *steadfast* will I make a pillar in the house of my Lord and they shall go out no more." If you lack steadfastness, speak to yourself. Rub the back of your neck and say, "I dare, I dare with the fire of God, I dare."

Here is the sad thing. When people take LSD or other street drugs, the center of enthusiasm is damaged. Also, alcoholism damages this center. Look at people who take drugs. They are numb without the fire of the almighty God.

We are children of God. In us is the power of creative enthusiasm. No longer shall it be dormant. We ask, "Oh Lord, touch us with your holy fire, make us sparkling, make us electrified by you, make us steadfast for you."

Mind Power Can Solidify into Matter

Matter can be crystallized energy, mind energy. In order to heal this crystallization, we have to first undo the coagulation on the physical level. Next, we bring it to the surface and examine it. Finally, we change our negative mind pattern to positive thinking.

Example:

If you are in pain, you cannot think positively.

If you are nauseated, you cannot have heavenly thoughts.

If you are injured, maimed or short of breath, you have to undo and nullify these things on the physical level, then try to do it on the emotional level. Then change your thinking.

Mental Clarity

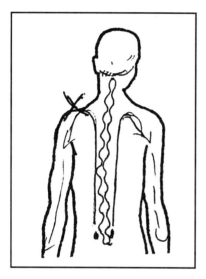

Place your left hand on the left shoulder of your brother. Start at bottom with one finger on each side of the spine and slowly move up. When you arrive on point x, draw your right hand under the left hand and both hands go down over the arms. Shake your hands and start again. Do this several times.

The Development of Thought Power

Acquisition of Thought Power by Moral Purity

A man who speaks the truth and has moral purity has always powerful thoughts. One who has controlled anger by long practice has tremendous thought power.

Thought Power by Concentration

There is no limit to the power of human thought. The more concentrated the human mind is, the more power is brought to bear on one point. Cultivate attention and you will have good concentration. A serene mind is fit for concentration. Keep the mind serene. Be cheerful always. Then you can concentrate. Be regular in your concentration. Sit in the same place, at the same time, 4 a.m.

Thoughts can Promote Radiant Health

The body is internally associated with the mind, rather the body is a counterpart of the mind; it is a gross, visible form of the subtle, invisible mind. If there is pain in the tooth or in the stomach or in the ear, the mind is at once affected. It ceases to think properly; it is agitated, disturbed and perturbed.

Napoleon controlled his thoughts in this manner: "When I want to think of things more pleasant, I close the cupboards of my mind revealing the more unpleasant things of life, and open up the cupboards containing the more pleasant thoughts. If I want to sleep, I close up all the cupboards of mind!"

If the spoken word has to have power, it has to have enthusiasm. The sound of the spoken word affects the thyroid gland, then the thymus gland and the spleen. The thyroid, thymus and spleen are the center of the immune system. Therefore, the spoken word is a constructive rebuilder.

The wave of the spoken word goes on in the pineal gland, stimulating it, then to the pituitary gland, balancing it, then on to the saliva glands, the solar plexus and the adrenal glands. Every center in our body is affected by our speech. It intensifies or dissipates our aura.

The power of the spoken word is not only for yourself, it also is for others. Every time we speak, we send out sounds through our etheric, astral and mental centers. This is the mechanical way a spoken word goes. On its way to the aura, it stimulates or depresses all glands. The spoken word uplifts or destroys.

III. EMOTION

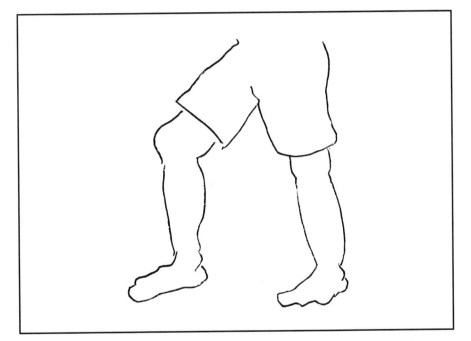

When you know where you are going,
the world steps aside.

III. EMOTION

The Chemistry of Emotions

Anger

Fear

Removing Harmful Emotions

Freeing Yourself

The Chemistry of Emotions

At the National Institute of Mental Health in Bethesda, Maryland, research is under way that could enhance our understanding of the mind/body relationship.

Dr. Candace Pert, Ph.D., chief of the institute section on Brain and Biochemistry, stated, "Emotions are not just in the brain but are also in the body and appear to run the immune system, the glands, the intestines. So your whole body is a single-unit integrated circuit, running on biochemicals." Once all of this is fully understood, it may provide the medical profession with totally new ways to treat diseases such as cancer, schizophrenia, obesity and AIDS.

Upset Emotion

Upset emotions can have visible manifestations in the following disease patterns:

- Toxic condition in lymph
- Toxic condition throughout the body
- Skin condition
- Hair loss
- Paralysis
- Metabolic disorders

We have two important glands for decongesting emotions. The first is the pineal gland. This gland is the master gland. It is located close to the pituitary gland, in the middle of the brain, a short distance behind the root of the nose. This gland, when well developed, brings emotional and physical well-being. This gland is also the throne of our faith. As we develop faith, we develop the pineal gland. Faith alone has no power. So God gave us another gland right next to the pineal gland. It is the pituitary gland. The pituitary gland lies in the "Turkish saddle," well imbedded, and is the gland of imagination.

These two we may call twin glands. We can imagine that some kind of healing without the power of faith will not bring lasting results. On the other hand, faith—blind faith—without the goal of imagining, has no end result and will not open the doors for healing the body. For example: Someone is confined to a wheelchair or is bedridden. The first thing this person has to do, and with him all people concerned, is to imagine that he/she can walk again. See them walking, see them well, see them placing the foot on the floor. And then believe what your mind sees. You cannot tell what comes first, imagining or faith. Both are needed for results.

First question: How can we strengthen these mentioned glands, these powerhouses? Next question: How can we line up these glands so they work together? In this book are some suggestions which worked well for me and others.

The first gland affected by emotions is the thyroid gland and with it the parathyroid gland and then the thymus gland. The thyroid gland and thymus gland are part of the immune system. With the spoken word you influence your immune system right now.

It is known that in times of grief, people get viruses, the flu and other infections. They say the cemetery was cold and windy or, in the chapel during the service, people were coughing and crying and spreading germs. The truth is that the power of the spoken word of sadness has depressed the immune system to an extent that people could not throw off the germs which were dormant in their system.

What to do

Close your left eye.

With your right eye look into a mirror and stare into your eye's image and say, "Flu, you are gone. Get out of me right now." Repeat several times. You will be amazed!

An emotional crisis does more than injure your psyche. It jeopardizes your physical health, it increases your risk of sickness and it can add to accidental injuries.

How can that be? Under stress, the normal immune system defense can break down, resulting in greater readiness to disease. Colds, the flu, mononucleosis and even leukemia can be triggered by an emotional crisis.

What to do? Don't be passive. We all go through difficult times. We feel helpless, hopeless and overwhelmed. Take on a positive approach. I would say that an active approach is to DO something!

Problems always come in pairs or clusters. I personally make a list of the problem or problems I am confronted with. After writing them down, I read each one and think them over and cut out the problem that can be solved the easiest. Then I go to the next one and down the list until I find one or two at the core, so to speak, at the center of the stress.

By unwrapping the problems in this manner, one can intelligently and almost totally solve the emotional stress which can make you sick.

Nervous Disorders

Many people with nervous disorders have fallen arches. I notice that many cases involving insecure walking are accompanied by fallen arches. The following work will help to bring fallen arches back to normal position and clearer thinking is the result. To bring arches back, apply pressure on center peroneal group of muscles (see demonstration).

See also Ch IV (Key Positions: Nervous System) and Ch. VI (Inner Organs: Nervous Breakdown).

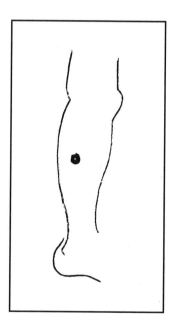

The Importance of Dealing with Emotions

How is it possible that feelings of anger, jealousy, hostility and fear can affect our health? Are these feelings not just a passing situation? Unfortunately not and I explain this in short.

When we are in a threatening situation, the stress hormone (adrenaline) and its companion (noradrenaline) are poured out in great quantities. These hormones stimulate the brain to quick and immediate action. From there the excess reaches the arterial system and adds to the formation of plaque buildup. The cortex of the adrenal gland is stimulated by resentment, jealousy or feelings of defeat and releases a hormone called cortisol. This would not be dangerous in small doses, however, prolonged resentments and affiliated feelings put so much cortisol out that your health is threatened from within.

Why is that? Cortisol is released by the cortex of the adrenal gland. Too much cortisol diminishes the power of the immune system by depressing the natural killer cells. Natural killer cells are watchdogs of the immune system and destroy dangerous and abnormal cells as needed. When too many abnormal, fungus-type cells take over, these fungus-type cells may develop into tumors.

Another bad thing about uncontrolled, prolonged emotions and emotional stress is that the precious interferon cannot be manufactured and T cells and B cells have no nourishment.

We live in a stressful world. What can we do to stay emotionally sound?

- Examine your problem.
- Singing in groups in churches or by yourself reduces and releases emotional stress.
- Recite a poem.
- Physical exercises help tremendously.
- Look at a problem with a humorous outlook. In every problem is something funny.
- Believe in something sacred and holy or in things that stimulate happiness and thankfulness.

Anger

Emotions are a great force for either good or, if not controlled, evil. Let us go over some aspects of emotions.

Anger can be a holy anger. Christ took his whip and cleared the temple from the cheating merchants. Anger can arouse a person to tremendous powers.

- A middle-aged woman saw two huge men molesting a young girl. The girl screamed but no one paid attention, no one wanted to entangle with these men. The woman got so angry that she took her umbrella, opened it and rammed it into one of the fellows. He fled and so did the other crook.

- One young man started a business. It looked as if it would fail. Neighbors and relatives laughed and said, "You are a failure to begin with." He got so angry that, in spite of all the odds, he made it and he made it big.

- Two fellows started a fist fight of a serious manner in front of my little store. The huge window pane started to quiver back and forth. I got so angry I took the broom and beat them up with the broom and so saved my window and stopped the fight.

When we can arouse a cancer victim to anger about themselves and the situation, we almost have won the battle. A cancer victim needs that holy sword of anger and they are able to heal themselves.

A person with paralysis does not need sympathy, they need the holy sword of anger. It will knit the nerve connections. They have to do it for themselves and they will succeed. By the way, take them out of the chair and let them crawl on the knees. Below the knees is the entrance to the central nervous system. When treated this way, it repairs. No wonder the churches had such results. They put their holy shrines way up on the mountains. The ones seeking help had to crawl up on their knees. There was no car or horse carriage and, wonder over wonder, when after hours or even days they arrived, their ailments were gone.

When anger is not released, it turns into resentment. It can turn into violence, it can turn into destruction, particularly for the one that carries it.

Release Anger and Resentments

See Ch. I (Soul Level: Resentments) for instructions on how to release anger and resentments.

Fear

Another aspect of emotion is fear. Fear paralyzes. If I see a snake, I stand still from fear. If you are afraid, your T cells in the immune system freeze up. They stand still and close up and your immune system goes way down.

I have an easy way to overcome fear and you will laugh at it but it works. Pinch your buttocks—pinch them hard—and all fear is gone.

Love is an emotion. You may have self-love or you may have the attribute of God which is true love and this will open for you the doors of great happiness of light and healing.

What to do

What can be done? How can we keep the connection between the thymus and heart open? Pound your breastbone for 1 or 2 minutes, then continue doing so and start rolling your head. Do both pounding your breastbone and rolling your head at the same time for 1 more minute. Soon you will feel warmth coming to your heart, you'll start yawning or sighing (or both) and an unaccountable happiness will spread over you. The secretion of the thymus in an adult makes an etheric stream and increases intelligence, self-esteem, happiness and trust. In addition, the herb thyme is very valuable to keep the thymus gland in good shape.

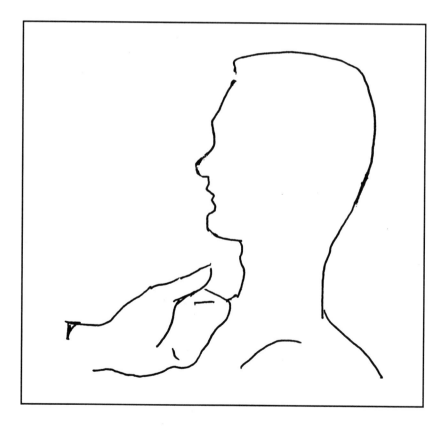

Removing Harmful Emotions

Hold points 1 and 2 for 60 seconds. Hold points 3 and 4 for 60 seconds. Do this 2 times daily.

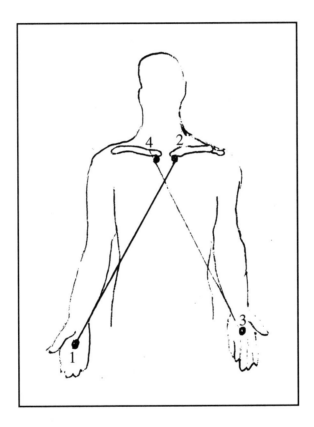

If you find your trouble in column I, a possible solution could be found in column II.

I		II
Throat	=	Fear
Heart	=	Emotion
Ears	=	Obedience
Eyes	=	Obedience
Fingernails	=	Aggression
Feet	=	Steadfastness
Gallbladder	=	Freedom power
Knee	=	Submission
Lung	=	Communication
Stomach	=	Feeling
Mouth	=	Acceptance
Muscles	=	Activity
Blood	=	Life force, vitality
Kidney	=	Partnership

If in shock, pound the sternum.

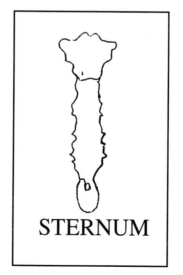

STERNUM

Freeing Yourself

This is my story on the subject of freeing yourself. In May 1953, our family arrived as refugees in America. We brought along 5 children, several sacks of old clothes, some tools and feather beds all packed in a tin bathtub. I thought that we had to start out like the old settlers in the wilderness and I wanted to be sure my children got a bath once a week. I did not know that America was so highly civilized.

I had carried myself well but once we had settled down, my husband, an engineer, had found work and I went house cleaning. Something was bothering me. Every night, night after night, I was reliving the past. The nights of terror, the bombing, the hopelessness, the uncertainty if my husband would return from captivity in Russia. I was exhausted in the morning. I felt my health slipping. My first cousin was a psychiatrist in Milwaukee and I asked her what to do about it. She gave the following advice: "Here is a paper and a pen. Every night when you are alone, sit down and write out what you experienced. Don't read it over. Put the writing in a the drawer. Next morning read it and burn it. Do this for a week or until you have nothing to report to yourself."

I started that very evening. After a week, I was free. I was free from the old stuff that was hindering me to start a new life. Every morning when I reread the written notes, it was like a fictional story.

I went back to my cousin and thanked her and asked "Elizabeth, how did this work? Why did this work? I had tried so many things but this worked."

She answered, "As you speak your troubles out, they become larger, bigger, tremendous, voluminous in size, but when you write it out and read it the next day and burn it, it takes on a different dimension. It is out of your brain, it is out of every cell of your body and you are free and can stay well."

Thank you forever, Elizabeth. I have given this formula to many, many troubled people and troubled souls and every time it works.

Free yourself from the old pattern and you open yourself to new and better experiences. My health had returned in one week and so will yours. Try it.

This knowledge is particularly important after a painful divorce. Make yourself free from a terrible nightmare of guilt and start anew. It is often the case that men and women remarry and find the same situation as they had left behind. Why is that so? It is because they had not freed themselves. The way it was shown to me by a psychiatrist is the surest way to total success.

IV. KEY POSITIONS

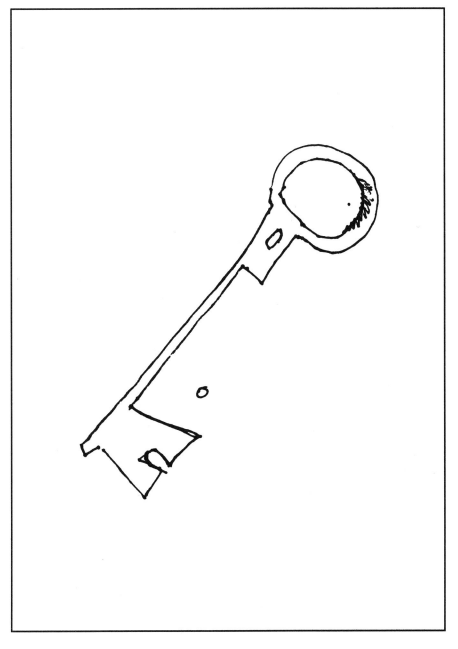

IV. KEY POSITIONS

Hands

Skeletal System

Ligaments

Muscles

Lymphatic System

Venous System

Blood

Lungs

Exhaustion

Nervous System

Brain

Ovaries

Our bodies are composed of different systems. These systems have to work together. When one system is diseased, all systems suffer. When the blood is sick, the transportation of life force is interrupted. When the decalcification of the bones takes place, everything suffers. Each of these systems has a master key, a point by which the systems are influenced. Holding a point will influence a particular system. The key positions of the following systems are known.

Hands

Your hands are shaped like His, and so
Be careful in the things they do.
Let them be quick to lift the weak,
Let them be kind and soft and strong.
May they be swift to heal the sick,
To ease a load . . . to right a wrong.
Your hands are made like His. Beware!
They hold the weight of no man's pain,
Why asked their aid to help him bear
His suffering . . . and asked in vain.
He made the deaf to hear . . . the lame
To walk . . . the blind to see,
Until one day the fools they came
And nailed His hand upon a tree.
Our hands are like His hands. As wings
Let them caress all living things . . .

Skeletal System

Hold the seventh cervical vertebra. Do not rub, do not manipulate, just hold. It will influence favorably and heal the entire system. If you have broken a bone this point will be sore but it also will heal any bone in the system when you hold it long enough. The rule is, hold this point for 3 days in a row (a friend may have to help hold for you) and your bone is healed. For the elderly it will take 6 days to accomplish this.

Comfrey Root Tincture
Bone strengthener, bone pain, broken bone, stump pain. Take 5 drops in water. Also 1 drop on seventh cervical vertebra.

Ligaments

The key position for the ligaments (all ligaments in the body) is a point above the elbow of your right arm. Open your hand. From the thumb upward, over the elbow and directly on the bone, you will find a sore spot. Hold it for 60 seconds. It will hurt when needed. You will feel the ligaments going into place wherever it was needed.

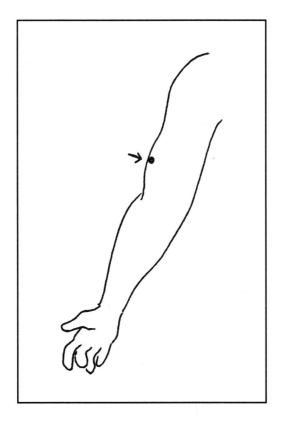

Dandelion Root Tincture
   Injuries to muscles, tendons. Make compresses and apply to point.

Muscles

The key position of all muscles in the body is below the calves.
Sit on a chair. Flex your knees and hold the point firmly until the
pain is gone.

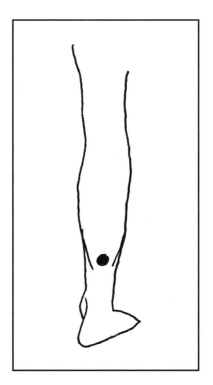

See also Ch. VIII (Muscles and Tendons).

Lymphatic System

The key position for the lymphatic system is as indicated below. Right hand straight into the left armpit, left hand held over seventh cervical vertebra. The fingers must be spread. Unbelievable results in all lymph disorders, including leukemia, lymphoma and swelling in any part of the body. Hold for 10 minutes, 3 to 4 times daily. Your friend will soon feel a tingling left hand, then left foot, then right foot, then right arm, then heart. The heart is not felt so hold a little longer after the right arm tingles. Some feel it as a warmth. The entire healing takes 3 minutes.

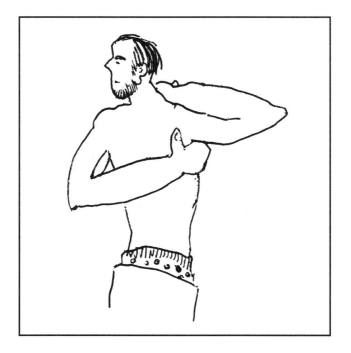

The lymphatic system becomes sluggish with a lack of exercise. In all cases of cancer, the lymphatic system should be stimulated. Do not make Swedish massage. In cancer patients it is too dangerous because cancer is easily transferred from one place to another. By stimulating these points, the lymph will carry out trapped garbage and trapped protein. *See also* Ch. V (Glands: Lymph Glands (Nodes)).

Venous System

To influence the entire venous system, hold the following points on the head. In the back of the head are two indentations (*see* diagram). Hold them for 3 minutes at a time, 2 or more times daily. You will be amazed that the protruding veins in your hands will vanish.

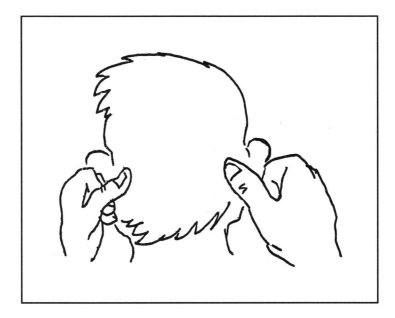

Blood

The key position for the entire blood system is the following: Person should lie on back. You stand on the right side of the body. Lay your right hand over the liver, the left hand folding skin and muscles over the right hand. Start below and move slowly upwards until you reach the stomach. Do this stroking and kneading 12 times, slowly and not harshly.

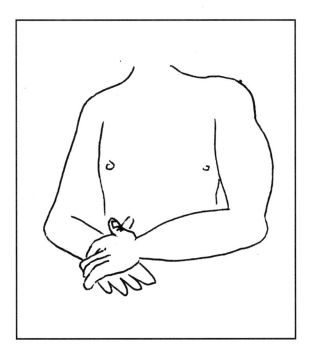

Lungs

The entrance key to the entire lung system is on your right side, between the second and third rib. Hold it and take a deep breath. Exhale in a forceful manner. Do this 7 times. It will stimulate the lungs.

Exhaustion

See Ch. I (Soul Level: Exhaustion) for the key position to exhaustion.

Nervous System

The key position of your central nervous system is below the knee (get on your knees).

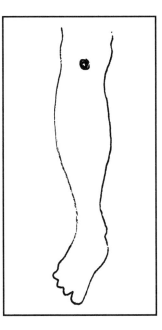

The nervous system is composed of two systems:

1. The central nervous system

2. The autonomic nervous system

The central nervous system has its keys below both knees. If your central nervous system is in trouble, as in back injuries or paralysis, start rubbing the places below your kneecaps. As soon as you can, get on your knees and start "walking" on your knees. In the beginning it is very awkward and painful but soon your central nervous system will respond. In some churches, kneeling benches are installed. These are very helpful to bring the central nervous system into action. In Europe, healing shrines are placed on high places and there is no road for cars to go up there. People have to go up walking. Better yet, they are instructed to crawl up on their knees. When they arrive after hours, they are healed.

See also Ch. VIII (Muscles and Tendons: Paralysis).

Keys for Nervousness

First press outside of both legs. Underneath the knee you will find an indentation which is called the point of heavenly tranquillity. Press for 5 seconds. Next press on the middle of skull and count 5 seconds. Next press on the back of skull on both sides and count 7 seconds. Next hold behind both sides of the jaw and count 10 seconds. Cross arms and hold points as indicated in the second diagram and count 10 seconds. Do this 2 times daily.

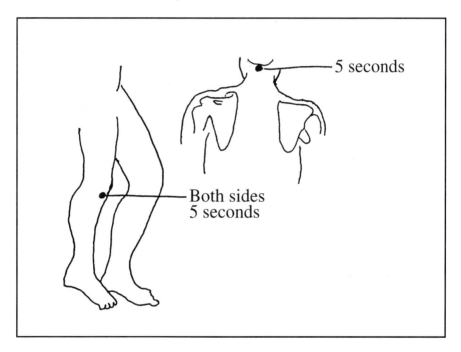

5 seconds

Both sides
5 seconds

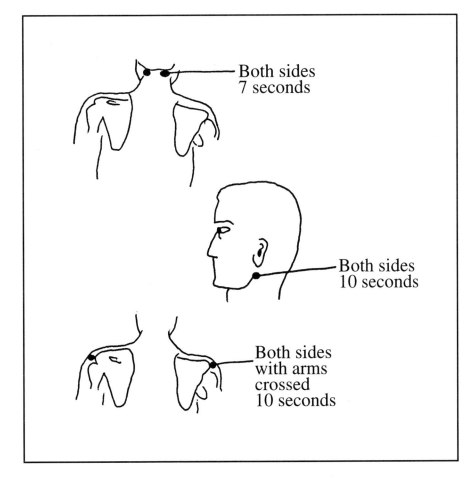

Both sides
7 seconds

Both sides
10 seconds

Both sides
with arms
crossed
10 seconds

Emotional Nervous System

The key position of your emotional nervous system is 1 inch below the breastbone. Hold until you feel a deep release, sometimes accompanied with a cracking sound.

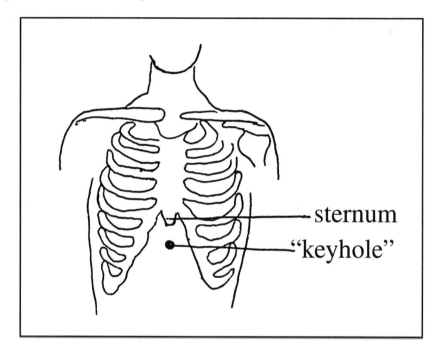

See also Ch. III (Emotion: The Chemistry of Emotions) and Ch. VI (Inner Organs: Nervous Breakdown).

Brain

Key position for the brain (3 times daily).

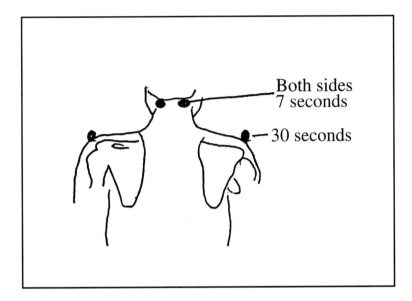

Ovaries

Key position for the ovaries. Heal your ovaries by holding the points indicated in diagram. Very valuable in cases of tubular pregnancy. In that case, someone else should hold for 15 minutes. Apply *Black Cohosh Tincture*.

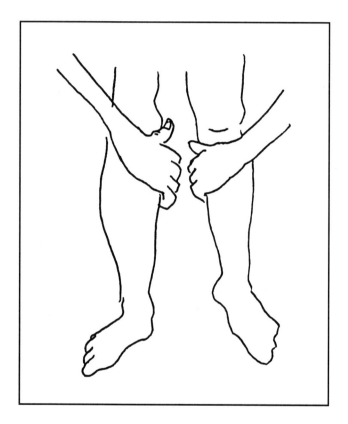

V. GLANDS

There is nothing hidden
that shall not be revealed
and nothing secret that
shall not be known.

V. GLANDS

Pineal Gland

Pituitary Gland

Thymus Gland

Thyroid Gland

Spleen

Lymph Glands (Nodes)

Tonsils

Breasts

Adrenal Glands

Pancreas

Pineal Gland

To stimulate the pineal gland, hold points as indicated for 30 seconds 2 times daily.

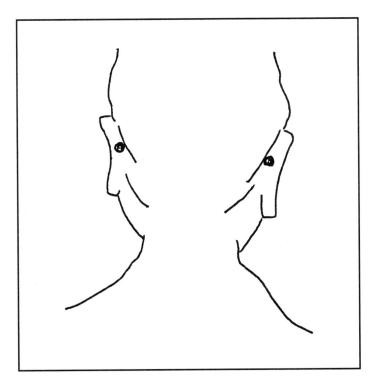

Wild Cherry Bark Tincture
    Food for the pineal gland—7 drops 2 times daily.

Pituitary Gland

The pituitary gland is your master gland which controls the complex functions of your body. It is located in the middle of the head just below the brain. The output of the pituitary hormones control:

- The chemical balance.

- The nerve impulses from the neighboring part of the brain called the hypothalamus.

- The endocrine system and its secretions of hormones and enzymes.

This tiny gland with its surrounding controls heartbeat, blood pressure, temperature and the functions of the body which are not subject to conscious awareness. This pituitary gland with hypothalamus is the go-between for intellect/emotion and body functions.

To stimulate the pituitary gland, hold for 30 seconds:

- Forehead

- 1 inch below breastbone

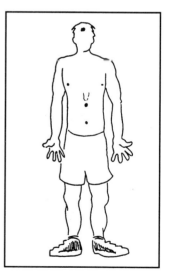

Thymus Gland

The thymus gland is located behind the breastbone. This gland is next to the master gland, the most important gland in the body. The lower part of the thymus gland touches the upper part of the sac in which the heart pulsates. The thymus influences the sensitivity of the heart. In fact, the thymus and heart are sympathizing with each other. The thymus gland is the seat of the ethical and moral understanding of a person. When we become mean, this gland stops working and doubt, fear, unethical behavior and despair set in. The thymus contributes to the inner faith, love and strength and enriches our lives. Sodium fluoride causes the thymus to malfunction and this adds to destruction of the inner values such as faith, respect, free will and hope. A child is born with a well functioning thymus gland. It is happy, trusting, hopeful and loving. The thymus and heart work together. As a person gets older, nothing is done to keep the thymus gland working. It barely makes the necessary hormones and secretions.

> ## The thymus gland is the main gland to bring the famous immune system to work.

The thymus gland excretes special hormones. With these hormones all glands benefit. All glands need a booster and that is what a healthy thymus gland does.

To strengthen this gland, beat the breastbone lightly with your fist and roll the head back and forth, up and down. Thyme tea is highly recommended. Please stay away from waters and items containing sodium fluoride. Sodium fluoride has a direct controversial vibration on the health of the thymus gland.

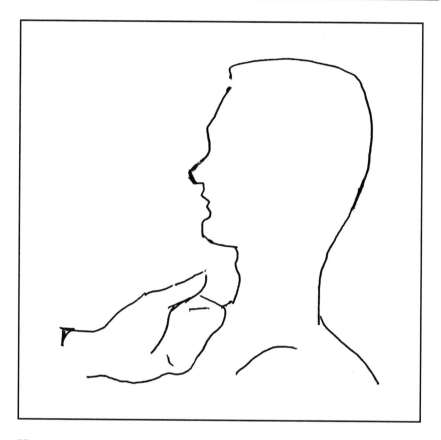

Here comes something very exciting. In my quest and search on how to improve ourselves, I found an article written by physicians in 1900. This article speaks about the thymus gland.

The thymus gland has its ganglion to the back of the neck and from there to the brain along the fifth and sixth nerves connecting eyes, ears, nose and heart.

The thymus gland, when working correctly, gives us faith, trust, confidence, understanding and clarity. As we get older the thymus gland shrinks and rigidity sets in.

Rigid neck muscles   =   Caused by shriveled up thymus
Rigid eyes   =   Cataracts
Rigid ears   =   Hearing problems

In the spiritual realm, it makes rigid dogma—lack of confidence in the goodness of our Creator, lack of confidence in ourselves. If the thymus functions normally, there is no such thing as a lack of courage, dissatisfaction or faultfinding.

What to do

1. Pound it, massage it.
2. Use the *Crystal Laser*.
3. Vibrate it, rub it in a circular motion.

It will take 9 months to revive it.

Thyroid Gland

I bring to you some interesting facts. The thyroid regulates the energy in cells and balances the cells as needed. The thyroid gives us material to strengthen our happiness, self-esteem and hope. A slow acting thyroid can be the cause of bones that will not heal. The face muscles sink in. Also, forgetfulness sets in. The interest in everyday doings diminishes. The voice becomes weak.

Low thyroid can contribute to:

• Hayfever
• Asthma
• Throat irritation
• Loss of voice
• Stomach trouble
• Constipation

Thyroid Stimulation Method

Have your patient sitting up for this application.

Right side application:
The operator stands on the right side, places the patient's left hand on point A and patient's right hand on point B. The healer does the same with his hands to supplement the energy. Hold these contacts for about 1 minute.

Left side application:
Get patient to do the same on his left side, placing his right hand on point A on left side and his left hand on point B on left side. The healer places his hands on patient's hands as well. Hold for 1 minute.
See also Ch. VI (Inner Organs: Thyroid).

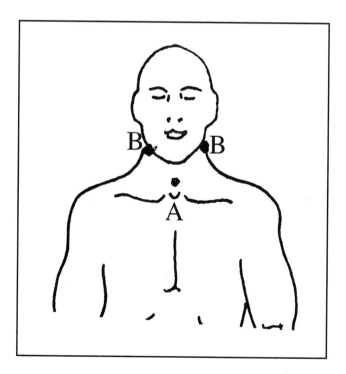

Spleen

The spleen is a very important organ. No wonder God planted it so deeply into our bodies so nothing can happen to this delicate organ. It is the only organ in the body which has two auras. It also is the only organ to be in complete yin-yang balance.

I have studied every available book on this subject, the spleen. A blocked up, congested spleen is a mystery. It is a gland of inner secretion and once the ducts become congested, we are in severe trouble.

An enlarged spleen (greatly the result of congestion) is capable of raising the left rib cage visibly. There is very little pain connected with it but fullness and pressure. A sluggish, congested spleen can add to mental instability, depression and stupor. A congested spleen makes a yellow complexion and brown discoloration appears over eyes, cheeks and around mouth. It may affect the heartbeat and often people sigh a lot.

Weakness, disorientation and being afraid of people, cellars, darkness or closed rooms point to troubles in the spleen. People with spleen trouble seem to be more affected by haunted houses and foreign energy possessions and many are obsessed or possessed for years until a helping minister or a psychic steps in to release these poor people of their entities.

To open the congested areas of the spleen, the following method is extremely helpful: Stand at the head of your worktable or slightly at the left side of your friend. Place the fingertips of your right hand under the right armpit. Rest your left hand over his/her solar plexus. Hold your hands in this position until you feel heat or throbbing. Your left hand will feel it more distinctly. Watch the color coming into your friend's face. See the lines in the face smoothing out. Watch the dark discoloration go!

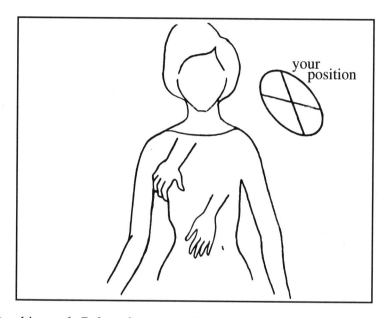

Do this work 7 days in a row. On the second day the patron may expel a sour, putrid stool, black or dark green in color.

Try this simple method on all mentally confused, epileptics or mentally exhausted and on your friends with blood impurities, acne, wrinkles or discolorations of skin in face and arms.

The spleen is the reservoir to store electricity of the body. If the spleen is not in order, the brain takes over this job. However, it has one drawback. People become egocentric. They accomplish nothing worthwhile.

Okra and red beets are revitalizing foods for the spleen.

Recipe:
>   2 qt concord grape juice
>   Juice of 6 oranges
>   Juice of 3 lemons

Cut the white of the lemon into small pieces. Boil this in a little water for 10 minutes. Add water to the drink. Then take distilled water and fill the liquid mixture to 1 gallon. This is 1 day's supply of your food-drink intake. Just 2 days of this will cleanse your organs as Drano cleanses your water pipes.

Lymph Glands (Nodes)

Congestion

The lymphatic system has many "pumps." If several of these pumps are stuck, they do not deliver the fluids to the special organs and so the organs are malnourished or toxic.

In this time and age, cancer is so widespread. Swedish massage therapy cannot be administered unless you know for sure your client has no cancer cells in the body. Otherwise, the cancer is spread from one place to another very, very quickly.

In order to influence the entire lymphatic system, the following treatment is needed:

Dr. Houston's Method

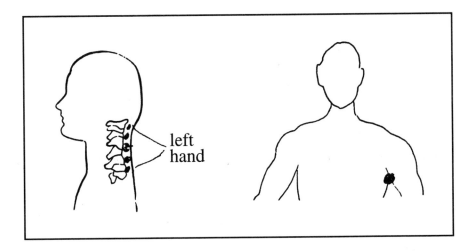

Spread fingers of left hand and rest on patient's neck. Make a spade with the right hand and go straight into the left armpit. Hold. Now relax and feel, imagine and direct with your prayers and your mind the proper flow of the lymphatic system. First, the left hand of your friend will become warm and cozy, then the left foot, then the right foot and then the right hand. You gave a complete massage without hurting in about 3 to 5 minutes.

When it comes to local lymphatic congestion, there are methods widely used. I demonstrate the most important ones. The lymph is a delicate matter. It should be handled gently, so lightly that you just touch the area in question and quiver your hand like a feather in the wind.

The entire lymphatic system is laced with filters—filters for the feet, tonsils, heart, arms and brain.

See also Ch. IV (Key Positions: Lymphatic System).

Sacred American Indian Treatment

- Operator has both hands open over patient without touching.
- Patient has both hands open.
- Operator moves hands slowly up and down.
- Patient moves hands slowly up and down.
- Operator moves hands slowly sideways.
- Patient moves hands slowly sideways.
- Operator goes behind ears and sways hands back and forth.

Operator goes to base of skull at the points behind the ears and opens lymph. Now operator goes down the spine with both hands at the same time on the right and left, ever so slowly, one finger ahead of the others.

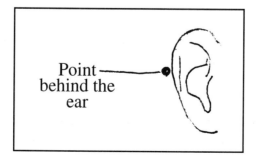

Point—
behind the
ear

Tonsils

Hold one finger on the tip of the collarbone. With the other hand, "milk" the lymph gland down with a very light touch. Do it from the ears to the clavicles. After finishing this movement about 10 to 12 times, take the other side and milk it down.

Usually the sore throat is totally gone and the tonsils start shrinking. Do it as needed.

Breasts

Breast lumps can be removed at an early stage, without surgery, by stimulating the lymph flow. Have the woman stand and have a second person, preferably the male energy of her husband, do the following (for purposes of this example we will assume the lump is on the right side):

1. Stand on the right side of the standing patient. Put the spread fingers of the right hand on the right side of the sternum where the breast tissue attaches. Simultaneously put the spread fingers of the left hand on the right side of the spinal column, approximately parallel with the right hand. Hold for 90 seconds. Prayers for healing are entirely in order through these stages by both the subject and the practitioner.

2. While holding the left hand in the same place, move the right hand to a position directly in the armpit with the spread fingers extending straight down out of the armpit. Again hold for 60 seconds.

3. Return to position 1. and hold for 60 seconds.

4. While holding the right hand in the same place on the right side of the sternum, shift the left hand to the position in the armpit and down from it. Hold for 60 seconds.

5. Return to position 1. and hold for 60 seconds.

6. Repeat this process 3 times daily until 3 days after the lump disappears. If the lump is on the left side, exchange the words "right" and "left" in the above instructions. If it does not disappear in 3 weeks, the case is more advanced and needs different care, including the possible use of magnets or fungus removing herbs. Of course, there is always the possibility the lump is something other than a blockage of the lymph glands.

Adrenal Glands

The following exercise will stimulate the adrenal glands and encourage them to produce more natural cortisone.

Stand with your heels together. Inhale deeply and fully, then hold your breath. While holding your breath, turn your head to the right until your neck muscles are pulled as taut as possible. This must be done without moving the body. Stretch until you cannot turn any farther, then hold to the point of dizziness.

Now exhale through the mouth.

Repeat this process 3 times on the right side, then 3 times on the left side. Each time try to hold the taut muscles just a little bit longer.

Pancreas

This large, elongated organ lies partially behind the stomach. It excretes 3 juices:

1. A digestive juice which flows into the duodenum.
2. Insulin for glucose digestion.
3. Alcohol for nerve and brain function.

In order to keep this organ in good condition the following method would be helpful: Lay on your back. Start "aura" massaging from the left side clear to the middle of the body. Do not touch the body. Keep hands ½ cm from the skin. Massage again and again for 5 to 7 minutes, then bring your hands to the right side and stroke, not touching the body, 12 times up the middle. Give your patron ⅓ tsp. of ground nutmeg in 1 cup of hot water and let him sip slowly. The blockage hindering the flow of fluid to and from the organ will be lifted and the organ will resume its work.

VI. INNER ORGANS

Life is given to us for the perfection of our nature
and thus the betterment of mankind.
The betterment of our nature
cannot occur without honest labor.

VI. INNER ORGANS

Hands

Rhythms

Pneumonia

Asthma

Breathing

Ear Stimulation

Kidney

Stomach

Itching

Bed-Wetting

Blood Clots

Sinuses

Thyroid

Cecum and Sigmoid Area

Dropped Organs

Ovaries

Liver

Liver and Gallbladder

Nervous Breakdown

Heart

Circulation

Eyes

Diaphragm Area

Hands

The hands are tools which the mind depends upon when it wants to get anything done. The laying on of hands has a wide range of meanings. The priests of old and the priests of today consecrated the laying on of hands which means laying on the "Hands of God." It is a very holy act in our churches. Ministers are ordained by the laying on of hands. Special gifts are conferred to individuals with the laying on of hands.

> ## The human hand is the antenna of the mind.

It is the hand which conveys the healing thought of the healer to the sick person. By this method, healing vibrations are picked up by the tissues, nerves and cells and quickly transfer the imprinted thought of health to other parts of the body.

If you have a telephone but do not speak into the speaker, the message will not be heard on the other side of the line. If you have a sick fellow man but you do not transfer your healing power of the hands through special "speaker places" on the body, the sick body cannot respond and cannot take the message.

The natural power, this healing element, is not limited to clergymen or priests. Nature gave mothers an unselfish readiness to help their offspring. In good and in bad days, mothers instinctively know what to do. They place their hand on the feverish forehead, they bathe the little bodies, they embrace the hurting, crying youngster.

Rhythms

You Can Heal

We all can heal, mainly ourselves. We all can help others to heal themselves. Doctors, practitioners, pharmacists, surgeons and healers can only give the supply needed so you can become whole.

To become whole, to be healed, is the work of the individual in need. Just as every art requires knowledge and practice, so does this art of healing require knowledge and practice. When you go to an art class, such as painting or wood carving, you will be instructed about materials as paint, canvas, wood and chisels. Whatever you create afterwards, it is the creative spirit in you which forms and you have the privilege through knowledge and practice to use your hands for creating new things and making old things new.

Circadian Rhythms Influence Organs

The biological clock that regulates day and night cycles is called the circadian rhythm. Besides color, the healing of congestion is rhythm. It is a tremendous healing factor. The heart heals under the rhythm of ¾, the lungs under the rhythm of ²⁄₄. The lymphatic system likes an even, soft rhythm like the sound and the rhythm of a brook in the forest.

Eat Light Food

- Rhythm of the heart: Every ½ hour give 4 oz of distilled water for 2 days.

- Rhythm of the kidney: Every 15 minutes give a small piece of watermelon or pear for 3 days.

- Rhythm of stomach and colon: Every 50 minutes give 2 oz of chlorophyll water for 3 days.

- Rhythm of the liver: Every 1½ hours give 10 oz limeade for 7 days.

- Rhythm of the pancreas: Every 45 minutes give ½ tsp. paprika in 2 oz pineapple juice. Alternate with papaya juice. Do this for 2 days.

- Rhythm of the nerves: Every 60 minutes give thyme tea and 12 manukka raisins for 1 week.

- Rhythm of the lungs: Every 2 hours give 1 cup linden flower tea and chew 2 small pieces of calamus root on the hour when you do not drink tea. Use it like chewing gum. Spit it out after you chew it. Do this for 3 days.

Pneumonia

The laying on of hands in pneumonia cases is the greatest joy that one can experience. Rest your right hand over the forehead of the one you want to give energies to but so that your finger rests in the middle of the nose. The left hand has to be placed on the back of the head so you really cradle the head. (The right hand in the front, the left hand in the back.) In this position, wait for 20 minutes. After 10 minutes, you hear it cracking and working in the chest. After 20 minutes, the afflicted one will breathe freely. Then place your right hand over the breastbone, fingers facing towards their chin, the left hand on back, and let more energies flow through, about 5 more minutes. Repeat as often as you think it is needed. Usually once is all it takes. With babies, do it as soon as the first signs of chest cold appear. Hold the baby in your lap and cradle its head.

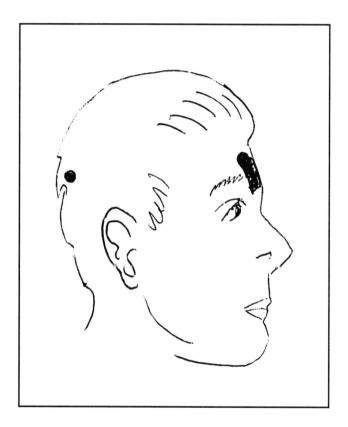

Asthma

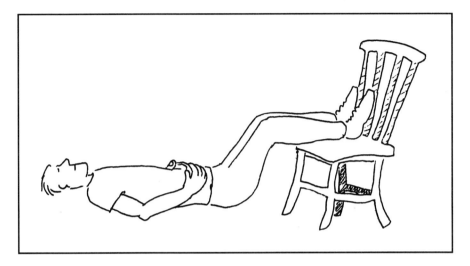

Let child or adult suffering with asthma lay on the floor. Bend the knees and elevate them on a chair. Hands should brush stomach from midsection right and left under the rib cage. Do it over and over, 10 minutes in the mornings and 10 minutes in the evenings.

One tsp. of cranberry concentrate opens the bronchi.

Breathing

Another Tool of Harmony in Breathing

When we breathe in we are closer to God, to the universal presence. As we breathe in we are receiving strength. As we breathe out we are releasing old stuff which we do not need. As we breathe in we should imagine a soft color such as pink, blue or green. As we breathe out we should exhale used up energies in darker colors. This will not only oxygenate blood but will also spiritualize being. Blood is the carrier of energies. Purified energies carry in with your breath and uplift your mind and soul.

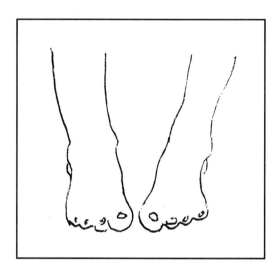

Note: Children and adults who walk with toes pointed inward are prone to lung diseases.

Ear Stimulation

This method will greatly assist in inner ear troubles and will also help in maintaining the balance.

Patient should lay on his back. Healer stands on right side of patient and places his right hand fingertips and thumb into patient's right hand. His left hand fingertips are placed on point No. 4. Hold the hands for 30 seconds to help energy flow.

Healer then moves over to the left side of the patient and places his left hand fingertips and thumb into patient's left hand. His right hand fingertips are placed on point No. 4 to complete the circuit. This is to be held for 30 seconds.

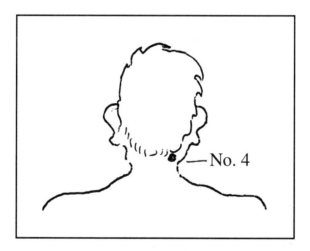

Kidney

The right kidney is positive magnetic in nature. Therefore, you have to place your left hand over the right kidney. The left kidney has a negative charge so your right hand has to be placed over the left kidney.

Have your friend lay on his stomach. Stand to the side of his head and let your hands rest on his kidney as I mentioned above.

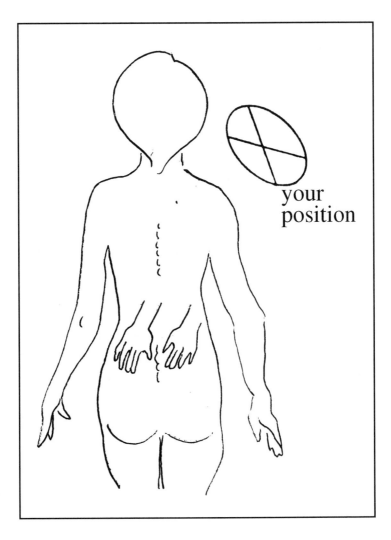

your position

Leave hands resting for 2 to 3 minutes, then slowly rotate your hands in the open loop manner towards the spine. The touch must be very light and do it only for 1 minute.

Finally, give the nerves on the spine a little twisting motion. For this you touch a little firmer and in a round circular motion. Let them know that they have to start working again. Just after repairing your wiring in the house you turn on the switch. It is the same thing here.

Stomach

The middle finger of your left hand rests in the "cup," the bones in front of the throat. Place right hand over stomach. Do not place it flat but form a cup out of your hand. Keep this hollow hand for 60 seconds, then make small, soft semicircles over the stomach. (Very good for underweight children and adults.)

Do this once daily for 7 days, then 2 times a week.

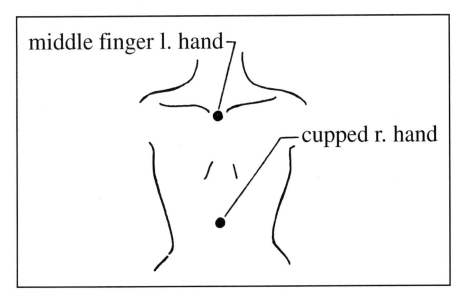

For Gas in Stomach

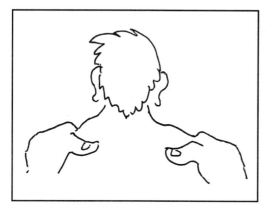

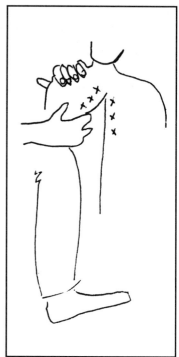

Lifting contacts x are made under both shoulder plates.

Raise and lower as gas is released all around shoulder plates. Most bad headaches are gas pressure to the head.

Itching

When people itch all over, the following treatment is of great value. Brush body from head to toe with your hands spread out and thumbs touching each other.

- Front 7 times
- Back 7 times
- Right arm 7 times
- Left arm 7 times

Also hold right hand over left shoulder. Brush with left hand the gall-bladder and liver area.

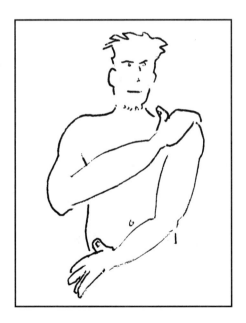

Bed-Wetting

Behind the ears are two tiny holes. Massage these holes with a very light pressure. At the same time ask someone to rub the feet with a towel until they are warm.

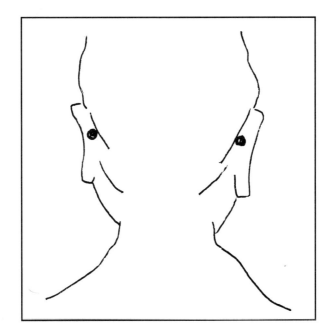

Blood Clots

Have your friend comfortable on the bed or worktable. Flex his knees. Have his hands folded as in prayer but his forefingers should form a pyramid. His thumbs close it. Cover your friend with a light blanket for warmth and comfort. There is nothing like a blanket pulled over you that gives you more security. Now sit on his left side. Spread your arms out so the right hand is over his head. The left hand is slipped under the cover. Hold it close to the tailbone. You cuddle your friend visibly and invisibly. Your hands do not touch the body at all but are 1 inch away from it.

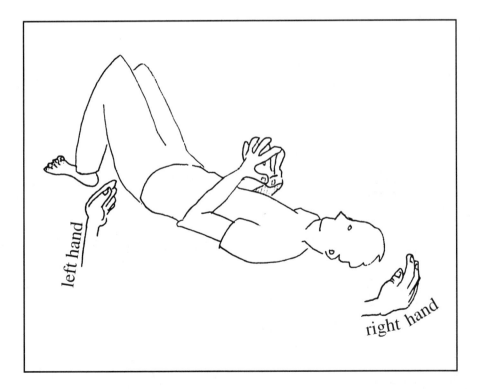

(The credit for this method goes to Rev. Dr. F. M. Houston.)

Sinuses

Hold as indicated.

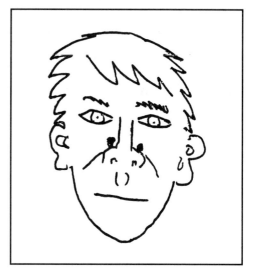

Thyroid

To stimulate, brush down 12 times, 2 times daily.

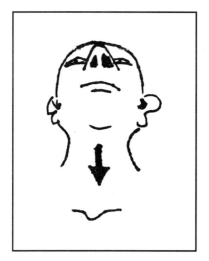

See also Ch. V (Glands: Thyroid Gland).

Cecum and Sigmoid Area

Stimulate cecum and sigmoid area with gentle lifting motions.

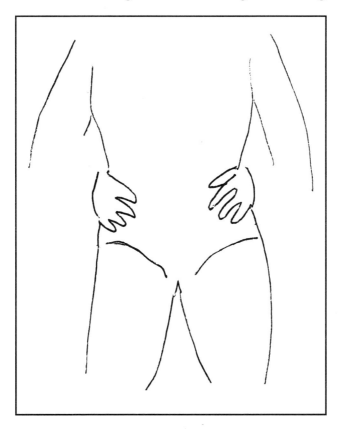

Dropped Organs

For dropped organs, lay on your back. Hold right or left point of the cup on the collarbone while you lightly sweep up the body (pray in Jesus' name that the organs move up). Then do the same for the left side, then do the middle. Sweep up until the pain is gone. When finished, suture by holding the ankles until your hand feels the pulse.

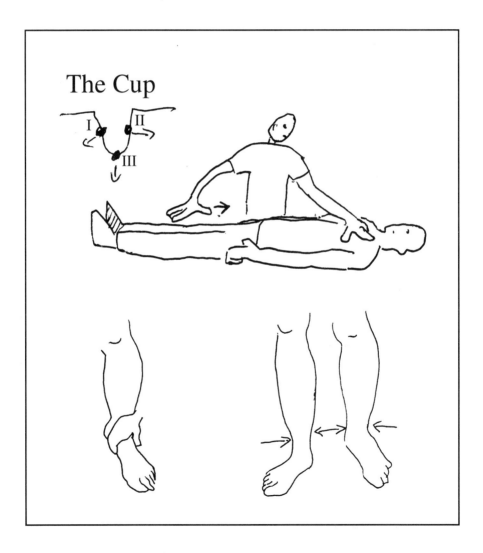

The Cup

Ovaries

See Ch. IV (Key Positions: Ovaries) for instructions.

Liver

Slightly, hardly touching the skin, rub in half moon fashion. Start at No. 1 and follow up until No. 4. Work slowly, take your time. After you do this 7 times, hold No. 5 as given in the drawing with your right middle finger. Do this firmly. The congestion will break up, sometimes with a gurgling sound. Also hold right hand middle finger and at the same time hold No. 6 under clavicle as shown.

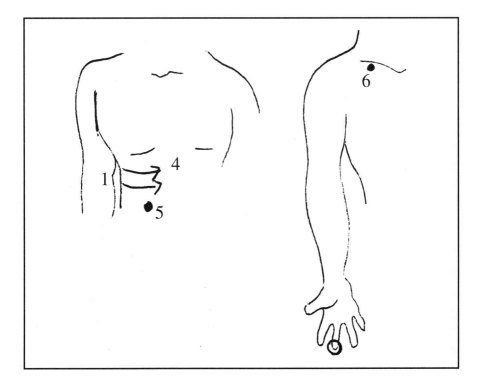

Liver and Gallbladder

Hold left hand on right shoulder. Brush with right hand 21 times from right side to middle of body (stomach).

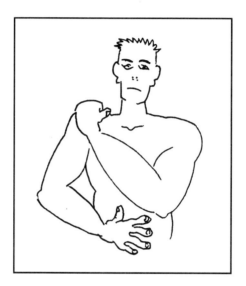

Nervous Breakdown

Many people with nervous disorders have fallen arches. I notice that in many cases of insecure walking people have fallen arches. The following work will help to bring fallen arches back to normal position and clearer thinking is the result. To bring arches back, apply pressure on center peritoneal group of muscles (*see* diagram).

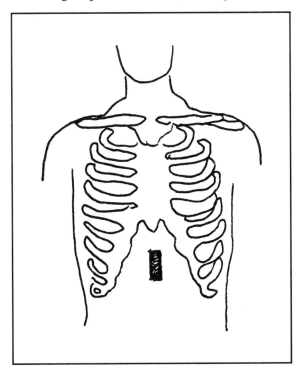

Applied to people with a nervous breakdown, it works like a charm. In all these severe cases, you have to hold this key position until it gurgles 3 times. Just before it gurgles, these people start asking for release of the pressure applied. Do not give in. Wait until it gurgles or snaps under your fingers. The pressure is firm but not torturing, not a light touch. It will take up to 20 minutes for the third release. Some folks start crying. Put a lavender colored cloth over their face so no one sees the tears and agony when the old pattern is released.

Folks who have had a nervous breakdown years ago also have to be released. And what a release it is for them! In some cases it is needed to "soften" the keyhole to the emotional body first. Apply lavender oil or eucalyptus oil on the keyholes under the knees and 1 inch below the sternum. Lavender oil is the best.

See also Ch. III (Emotion: The Chemistry of Emotions) and Ch. IV (Key Positions: Nervous System).

Heart

To calm down a rapid heartbeat hold right hand over the head. Touch with one finger. Hold left hand over thyroid. When you are emotionally troubled and you cannot sleep, try this method. It will calm you down and the relaxing sleep can come.

Hold sides as shown in this picture. It relaxes the heart muscle. Very important in heart attacks.

The spoken word influences the heart chamber. It opens it or closes it. It gives life power to the heart chamber or it makes it malfunction. If in shock by bad news, by a harsh judgment or by a word of fear, the heart chamber goes into spasms and it can be so strong, so powerful, that people faint, pass out or have a heart attack if conditions in the arteries are not right.

Take an herbal combination of:
- Hawthorn berries
- *Equisetum* concentrate
- Quaw bark

Circulation

To stimulate circulation place left hand on top of stomach, fingers pointing down. With your right hand stroke left leg with parallel strokes from the groin down over the left leg and over foot. Interrupt the magnetic lock by shaking hand and, in a wide semicircle, start at the groin down.

Eyes

This is used by American Indians: In the back of the head are 2 little indentations. Hold these with both thumbs for 1 minute. The first thing you notice is that the protruding veins on the back of your hand get smaller. Hold and the protruding veins will vanish completely. It has a profound affect on the eyes and brings circulation to the eyes.

Next, gently, gently touch the outside corners of your eyes and massage toward the eyes. This brings tired eyes to relax and will lubricate them.

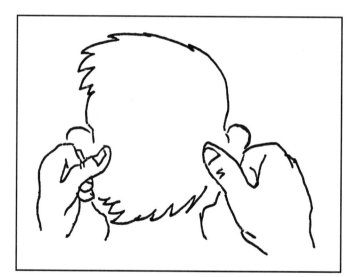

Then, in case of cross-eyed condition, massage the place indicated in the diagram. It has to be done very gently every day, 2 times daily.

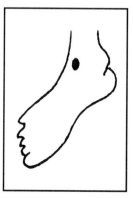

Lastly, in case of pressure in the eyes, as in glaucoma, the points behind the jaw release the fluid in the eyes. These points have to be held 10 minutes, 2 times daily for 3 to 4 weeks. Hold both sides.

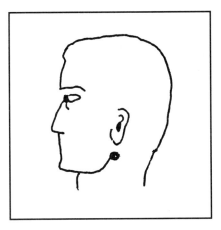

Diaphragm Area

This will help to give release to the rib cage on both sides and thus assist in energy breathing.

One will truly appreciate the relaxation this will produce on both sides of the chest area. It will also help to energize the gallbladder and the liver on the right side area and the spleen and pancreas on the left lower rib area.

These things may sound so simple but its effectiveness is what really matters.

Lay on your back. Put palm of right hand over liver, left hand on the neck area on the right side. Then place left hand over liver, right hand on left side on neck.

General energy circulation will take place within the organs concerned.

VII. COCCYX

In my opinion, this chapter is the most important chapter of the entire book. A misaligned tailbone not only gives physical troubles but it also adds heavily to psychological disorders.

VII. THE COCCYX: ITS ROLE IN THE HUMAN BODY

The Coccyx in Relation
to the Inner Organs

The sacrum and coccyx connect with the rectum, the prostate in men or the uterus in women (via Douglas' pouch) and, further forward, the bladder. These relationships are important in the treatment of many urogenital disorders.

The tailbone is surrounded by the anterior, posterior and lateral sacrococcygeal ligaments. In the normal subject, these ligaments allow good mobility while maintaining appropriate tension on the coccyx and associated structures. The coccygeal ligament is very important. It is the only manipulable ligament which enables one to have a direct effect on the dural tube.

Almost all of the soft tissue of the pelvis is attached to the coccyx. The connections are listed below to make you aware of the sacro-coccygeal articular lesion.

The waste of the lymphatic system and the waste gases of the nervous system leave the body via the tailbone. When the coccyx or tailbone is twisted, bent or injured, these gases are held as in a cup. When released, suddenly these waste gases are thrown against the diaphragm, causing severe sudden illness, often mistaken for a heart attack.

Much research has been done and the following interesting facts are revealed.

The coccyx is a *pump* which pumps fluids of
the bone marrow,
the spine,
the brain
and other encased internal fluids.

Why has the coccyx such wide ranging effects? Because it is a pump. Let us shed light on some happenings. At 2 or 3 A.M., you experience severe pain in the heart region. You are rushed to the hospital just to be told that it was a pseudo heart attack. You are told that you are anxious, upset and overworked.

What happened? The malfunctioning coccyx could not take care of the overwhelming nerve poisons dumped to be orderly taken care of and the heart was sent into spasms.

Fears, frustrations, phobias and depression tend to create excessive alkalinity over a period of time.

The cerebrospinal fluid and the sympathetic chasm join together by the vagus nerve. The trigger point is the coccyx, the tailbone. If the tailbone is out of balance, these emotions can take over and make life most uncomfortable for the sufferer.

Psychological Disorders

- In depression, always check sacrum and coccyx.
- In brain fog or loss of clarity, see if tailbone is in place.
- Poison in tailbone. *See below.*
- Parasites lodged in tailbone. *See below.*
- In leukemia, check tailbone.

Poison in Tailbone

- Lead deposit lodged in the tailbone hinders the coccyx—the pump—to full action. Lead deposit can cause epilepsy and other nerve disorders.

- Mercury iodide lodged in the tailbone is one of the causes of shaking.

- Nickel lodged in the tailbone can be the cause of pain all over the entire body. Sit on a small pillow filled with poppy seeds.

- Parasites lodged in the tailbone can cause insanity and lunatic behavior. Mix equal parts oil of wintergreen with oil of sassafras. Apply a few drops of this mixture to the tailbone. It will take several weeks to see results.

In all cases of leukemia, the tailbone should be checked and realigned.

This knowledge comes from Professor Dr. Brauchle. Professor Brauchle began using these nonmedical methods in Dresden, Germany. In one wing of a 2,000 bed hospital he worked with 25 patients per week, mostly children. Each week 25 patients would walk out perfectly healed. Not one died from leukemia.

Then and now, both science and medicine dismissed the results. They called these methods hocus-pocus magic, witchcraft or some kind of hypnotherapy. It is none of these. We call it the healing power of God. Over 5,000 people who had leukemia used these methods and continued living. They call it something wonderful.

During World War II this amazing hospital was destroyed along with the healing practice. Only 3 known people escaped with the knowledge in their heads. One, Hanna Kroeger, eventually moved to the USA, keeping the methods alive on a modest scale.

The realignment of the coccyx is not painful. You cannot make mistakes. It is not an osteopathic or chiropractic treatment. It stands all by itself as a vibrational treatment. When the tailbone is realigned, it gives a whooping spurt of energy to children.

How Can Coccygeal Problems Happen?

It may have happened with a fall on the coccyx bone many years ago, a car accident, giving birth to a child or other circumstances. This is what osteopathy is teaching us and they add in their books: This coccyx trouble had its effect on the kidney, bladder, lungs, stomach, heart and other organs. We do not understand this completely and more research has to be done.

Remember the coccyx is a pump for bone marrow and all other liquids encased in tissue of bones.

How Can You Align a Tailbone?

Put child on stomach and loosen the spine by light massage downward on both sides of the spine. Do it 3 times on each side.

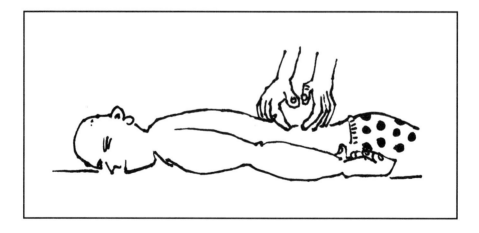

Turn your child's head so it is facing you. Hold one hand over sacrum.

Lift your child's leg, bend knee and bring it towards you, inside and back to the middle. Do this 3 times. Now 3 times outside and back to the middle. Then down and back to the middle 3 times. Then up and back to middle 3 times.

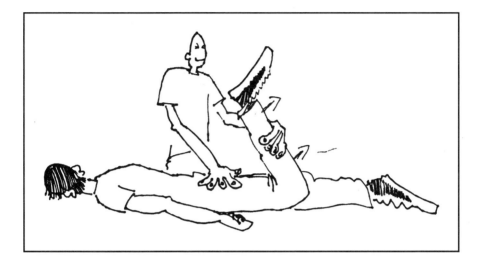

Now turn child's head. Repeat: 3 times inside, 3 times outside, 3 times down and 3 times up.

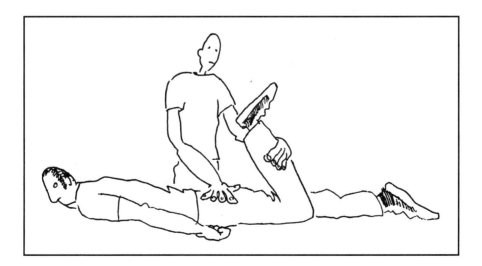

Now lift leg by sliding under thigh and swing leg towards you 1, 2, 3 times.

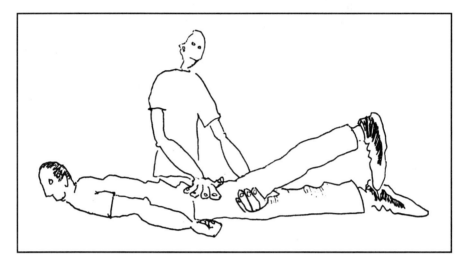

Now go to other side of the person and repeat all steps.

VIII. MUSCLES AND TENDONS

VIII. MUSCLES AND TENDONS

Hands

Accidents

Ligaments

Leg Cramps

Muscle Tone in Arms and Legs

Energizing Muscles

Paralysis

Abdominal Energy Release

Hip Tension Release

See also Ch. IV (Key Positions: Muscles).

Hands

See Ch. VI (Inner Organs: Hands).

Accidents

Always begin with accidents.

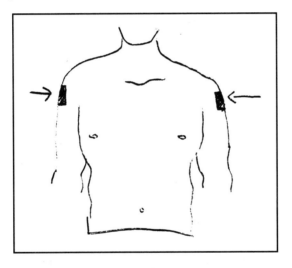

Hold points for 5 minutes. Feel release where accident had taken place. By holding these points accidents are released, even when they are of old, old standing.

Ligaments

See Ch. IV (Key Positions: Ligaments).

Leg Cramps

These contact treatments will greatly assist in all cases of leg cramping which usually occurs due to a calcium deficiency. The patient should lay on his back. The healer stands on the right side of the patient and touches his right fingers on the right side on point II and his left fingers on the right shoulder of patient. The same procedure is carried out with healer on patient's left side. He touches his left fingers on point III (left side of patient) and his right fingers on patient's left shoulder. Each is held for about 30 seconds.

Muscle Tone in Arms and Legs

Following this method will assist the muscle tone in both the arms and legs: The person should lay on his back. The helper will stand on the person's right side. The helper then places the right fingertips into the patient's right palm. He also places the left fingertips and thumb on the point as indicated.

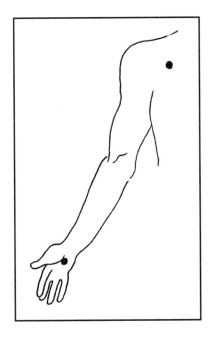

Energizing Muscles

Lower Limb Energizing

Place the palm of your left hand over the back of the patient's left knee and the palm of your right hand over the back of the right knee. If you want to give yourself a treatment, the same procedure can be done while seated, using your own palms to make the contacts behind your own knees.

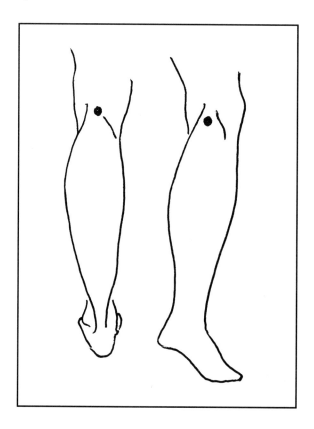

American Indian Method

Here are some methods the American Indians used. Stand on the left side of the person you want to give energies to. Take the middle finger of your right hand and place it under the skull of the right side of your patron.

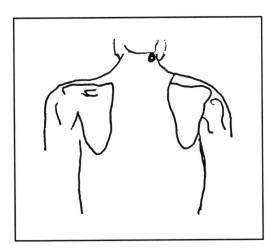

The left hand you place on the area you want to give energies to—a broken foot, a bellyache or wherever energies are needed. Hold it there for 5 minutes or until pain is relieved.

In order to increase the power, do the following: Stand on the left side of the person you want to give energies to. Place your middle finger of the right hand under skull as before. Rest left hand on solar plexus. Another person places his left hand over yours and his right hand over the hurting or injured body part. This method is excellent. The joining of powers triples and quadruples the healing action of the laying on of hands.

Paralysis

For paralysis in legs and in difficulties lifting the legs. Also after back surgery or in any kind of leg trouble such as not being able to come up from a chair easily.

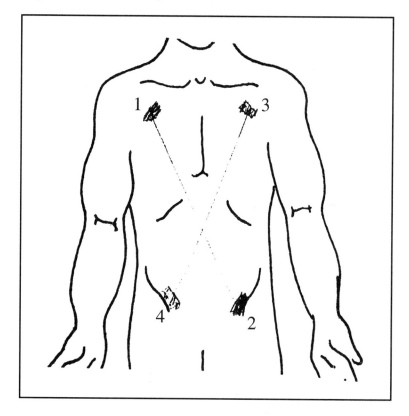

See also Ch. IV (Key Positions: Nervous System).

Abdominal Energy Release

The use of these contacts will release tension in the regions of the stomach, colon and small intestines.

The patient should lay on his back. The healer stands on the left side of the patient. He places his right fingertips on the left side about 2 inches from the navel. He then places his left fingertips behind patient's left knee. The patient can use his hands to do likewise to boost the energies—the left hand is held behind knee, however, the right hand moves one inch higher from the navel to make contact and then one inch lower than the first contact on left side of the navel.

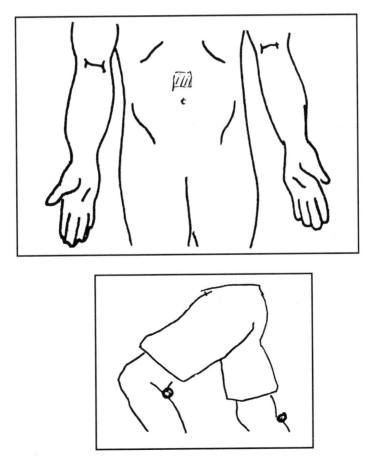

The same procedure is carried out with healer standing on the right side of the patient. The healer uses his left fingertips for abdominal contact on the patient's right side and uses his right fingertips to contact behind patient's knee. Procedure is the same as for the left side.

The abdomen will feel very relaxed and thus aid the energy from the abdominal brain (the navel) to become effective.

Hip Tension Release

Utilizing these contacts will assist in producing a marked relaxation of tension in the back of the neck muscles. Patient should lay on his stomach. The healer stands on patient's right side and places his right hand fingers and thumb on points I and II respectively. The patient can reinforce the energy of the healer or he can give himself the contact treatment.

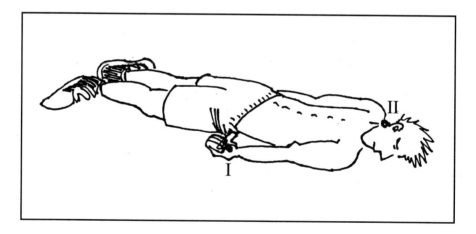

IX. SPINE

In order to accomplish anything, we have to have faith in ourselves. Very few people have faith in themselves. They like to put faith in other people and then they are shattered when other people do not live up to their expectations. Have faith in the power of God which lives in you. When we want to accomplish something, we have to have a definite goal. Remember, a true goal is a channel of service.

IX. SPINE

Disk trouble

Adjust ribs

Bring Clavicle into Balance

Hips

Whiplash

Align Knees and Ankles

Put Spine into Place

Mastoids

Carpal Tunnel Syndrome

Spiritual Alignment

Disk Trouble

St. John's wort oil remedy for disk deterioration: Have the person lay on their stomach. Have two people stretch the back. One person at the upper back stretches the muscles up towards the head, while the second person stretches the lower back muscles down towards the tailbone. Then rub St. John's wort oil on the spine, otherwise the adjustment will not hold.

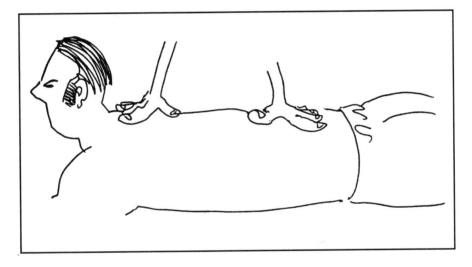

Adjust Ribs

Three people work together on this one.

First person with the rib out sits on a chair and relaxes. When the third person counts "1-2-3-UP!" blow out your breath on the word "UP." Not too deep of a breath but regular breathing. Do this 4 times.

Second person holds first person's arm at his side, elbow bent. While standing at the first person's left side, hold their bent arm with your left hand under their left forearm and put your right hand under their elbow. When the third person counts "1-2-3-UP!" lift up on the first person's arm. Do not pull the arm away from their body. Push up from the forearm and elbow points you are holding, so as to make the entire arm and shoulder raise 3 to 5 inches or so.

Third person, while standing on the right side of first person's body, places right four fingers on top of the rib cage near the center of the body on the chest. Then place left four fingers on the top of the rib cage near the spine on the first person's back. As you count "1-2-3-UP!" use a rotating motion by pushing with your right hand and pulling with your left hand to put the rib in place. This rotating motion may need to be done in the opposite motion as well, pushing with the left hand and pulling with the right hand, but not very often. Then move down the rib cage to a lower spot and repeat this motion 3 more times, each time going a little lower on the rib cage. Switch sides with the second person and adjust the other side of the body in the same manner.

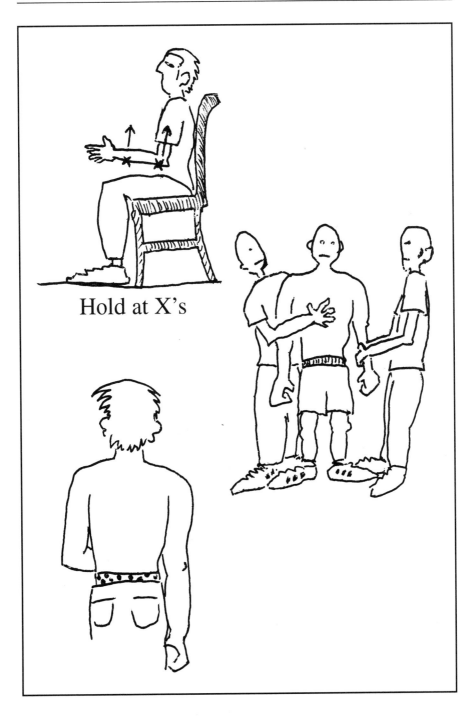

Hold at X's

Bring Clavicle into Balance

When the muscles on the inside of the arms are hurting, always remember the collarbone is out! In case you do not have a chiropractor, someone has to help you. Sit straight on a chair. Interlace your fingers and bring your arms to shoulder height. Place thumbs on points indicated. Your helper can do the job now. The helper slips underneath the left arm and holds the wrist. Now the helper swings you backward 3 times. Have the other side done 3 times also. If muscles in arms are still painful, repeat. Measure clavicles and you will find that they are straight.

Hips

The hips are so important because they are the foundation and the entire spine rests on them. If the hips are not in place, spinal adjustments will not hold for very long. Also, when the muscles which hold the spine in place have arsenic poisoning or cadmium poisoning, then the poison will bring the spine out of balance.

First determine the position of the pelvis. This is done on each side by placing the hand palm downward on the crest of the ilium. Now you know which is the low side, and which is the high side. You are ready to correct this.

Step 1—Separate your feet comfortably. Place your hand on the low side on top of your head.

Bend forward and rotate in a 45° arc. Go sideways and up on the side with your hand on top of head. Now shake hips back and forth.

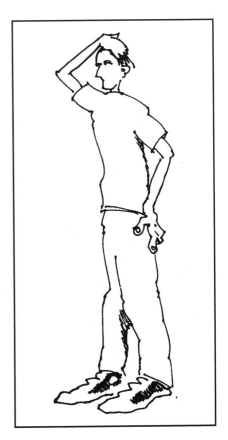

Step 2—Now, without moving the feet and keeping them apart, lift the toes of the high side and rotate on the heel inward to pigeon-toe the foot.

Now place the hand on the high side on the top of your head. Bend at the waist, forward, down, around and up, inscribing a 45° arc. Retrace this 45° arc back to center. Shake hips again.

Step 3—Place both feet together and make low side once more. Then, retrace this 45° arc back to center. Drop both hands to the sides. Shake shoulders back and forth. Measure your hips and you will find that they are O.K.

Whiplash

European method: Press body from the side with 50 lbs. pressure. Lift your friend just off the floor quickly. Go to other side and do the same. Whiplash is gone.

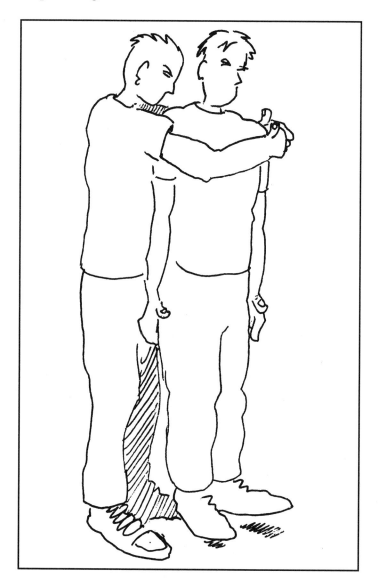

Align Knees and Ankles

With one hand, hold ankle. Bend the knee with your other hand. Lift leg to the middle and bend it inwardly with moderate pressure and tension.

First inside.
Then outside.

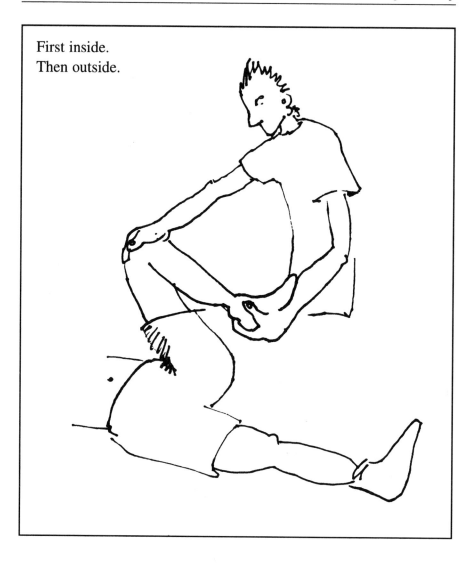

Then straight down.
Do this 3 to 4 times.

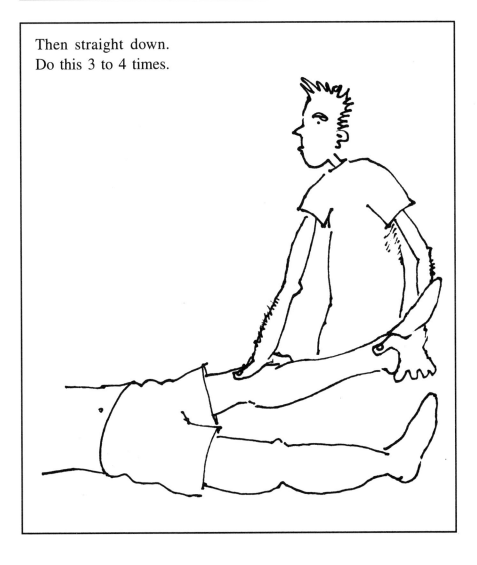

Put Spine into Place

Patron sits on chair, both hands on top of head. Move 45° forward, then right side and up. Move 45° forward, then left side and up. While patron moves, slide vertebrae into place.

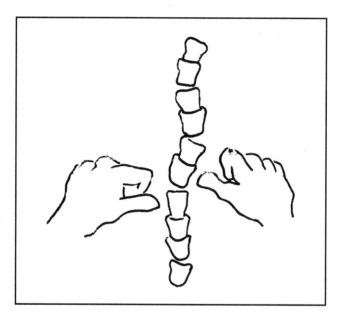

Mastoids

The mastoids have much to do with our hearing. The two mastoid bones are connected by tissue. This tissue extends forward making a connection with the inner eardrum. The outer eardrums, right and left, make connections with the mastoid glands which are directly behind them. These glands are not as noticeable in children as they are in older people. If there is an interference in the ears caused by the mastoid glands, it also interferes with our sight, taste and smell. In case the skull is deformed or out of order, it will bring pressure to bear on the mastoid glands, interfering with the medulla, and also affecting the senses of taste and smell. The seat of sight is located in the back of the head near the mastoid bones. If there is an unnatural pressure on this bone, it will dim the sight of the eyes.

In many cases of eruption in the mastoid bones, a fever or inflammation may appear. This causes a soreness of the bone behind the ear, causing an enlargement of the mastoid glands and, finally, interfering with the tongue and throat. One gland from each mastoid extends down the throat and attaches to the collarbone. A feverish condition of the mastoids may result in many disorders and throat trouble, causing large deposits of phlegm or mucous in the throat. You may recognize these conditions by a very bad odor of the nostrils.

This will be well appreciated by all patients who are unfortunate to suffer with sinus and migraine headache symptoms, loss of sight or loss of hearing.

Patient lies face down on the table and turns his head away from the helper. Helper stands on left side of patient, patient faces right. He holds patient's left thumb between his right thumb and fingers and places the fingers of his left hand on point 4 on the right side of patient's head.

Now ask the patient to turn his head to the left and healer commences treatment standing on the right side of patient. Healer takes patient's right thumb between the fingers and thumb of his left hand and also places his right fingers on patient's point 4 on the left side of patient's head.

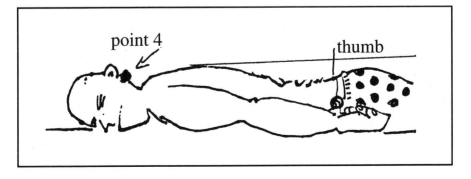

Carpal Tunnel Syndrome

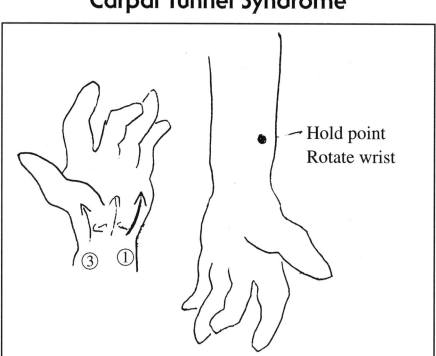

Hold point
Rotate wrist

Massage from small finger upwards. Move stroke by stroke upwards to thumb. Do this 10 times. Hold point and rotate wrist. The tensed ligament goes into place.

Spiritual Alignment

In my travels to teach this work of love, God sends me to the most wonderful places.

Once I met a dean of a chiropractic school. I talked about the impact of street drugs on the bones and that I can easily find out who is taking street drugs because of the shape the bones are in. I asked him for his opinion.

This is what this wonderful man said. Eighty-five percent of our bones are spiritual and respond to spiritual causes. Only 15% are material. He said, "When I am confronted with a serious dislocation, I go to another room. I take the chart of the spine and place the name or picture of the patient over it. Now I ask with the words of Christ for the spine to go in place. I go back to the patient and most of the job is done already."

I do it in the following manner: I lift up my left hand and ask that this hand of mine is filled with God's power. I take the index finger and the middle finger and slowly go down the spine while I am saying silently, "The cosmic all is the power of God's love. The cosmic all is the power of God's order." Do this 7 or more times in a row and people feel better.

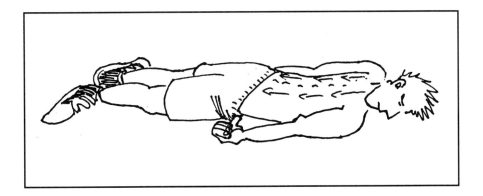

Don't forget to be thankful. Thankfulness is the expression of your soul. Thankfulness is the language of your soul. True thankfulness is rare. Even our Lord Jesus had to say a word about it. When someone is made whole, is "healed" and gives thanks, it is a seal, it is a covering, it is a protective veil that no other imperfection can get hold of them, that no other disease can destroy them. They have sealed the body against all negations.

When someone sends a thank-you note, I rejoice, for I know this person *stays healed* and stays well. Thank-you notes for Christmas are a request of your soul to give thanks to God, your beloved ones and your fellow man. Give thanks to the indwelling goodness of your fellow man. Also, by writing the cards, you straighten out your neglected self, your selfishness and, by doing so, you make yourself whole.

ABOUT THE AUTHOR

Hanna Kroeger, daughter of a German missionary, was born and raised in Turkey where she studied natural healing methods under the Oriental and European schools.

She studied nursing at the University of Freiburg, Germany, and worked in a hospital for natural healing under Professor Brauchle.

Hanna Kroeger is the founder and minister of the Chapel of Miracles and the owner of both Kroeger Herb Products and Hanna's Herb Shop. Through the little health food store in Boulder, she has been able to help thousands of people improve their health and well-being. She travels extensively throughout the nation lecturing and teaches at the Peaceful Meadow Retreat during the summer.

She has authored a total of eighteen books since the writing of this book, which is dedicated to the mothers of this nation whom she regards as the torchbearers for a healthier future America.

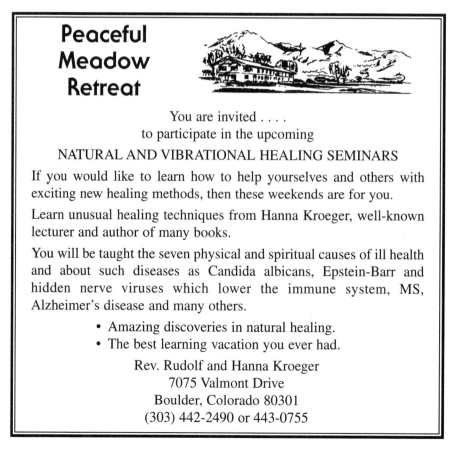

Peaceful Meadow Retreat

You are invited . . . .
to participate in the upcoming

NATURAL AND VIBRATIONAL HEALING SEMINARS

If you would like to learn how to help yourselves and others with exciting new healing methods, then these weekends are for you.

Learn unusual healing techniques from Hanna Kroeger, well-known lecturer and author of many books.

You will be taught the seven physical and spiritual causes of ill health and about such diseases as Candida albicans, Epstein-Barr and hidden nerve viruses which lower the immune system, MS, Alzheimer's disease and many others.

- Amazing discoveries in natural healing.
- The best learning vacation you ever had.

Rev. Rudolf and Hanna Kroeger
7075 Valmont Drive
Boulder, Colorado 80301
(303) 442-2490 or 443-0755

Books by Hanna

"Wholistic health represents an attitude toward well being which recognizes that we are not just a collection of mechanical parts, but an integrated system which is physical, mental, social and spiritual."

Ageless Remedies from Mother's Kitchen
You will laugh and be amazed at all that you can do in your own pharmacy, the kitchen. These time tested treasures are in an easy to read, cross referenced guide. (92 pages)

Allergy Baking Recipes
Easy and tasty recipes for cookies, cakes, muffins, pancakes, breads and pie crusts. Includes wheat free recipes, egg and milk free recipes (and combinations thereof) and egg and milk substitutes. (34 pages)

Alzheimer's Science and God
This little booklet provides a closer look at this disease and presents Hanna's unique, religious perspectives on Alzheimer's disease. (15 pages)

Arteriosclerosis and Herbal Chelation
A booklet containing information on Arteriosclerosis causes, symptoms and herbal remedies. An introduction to the product *Circu Flow.* (17 pages)

Cancer: Traditional and New Concepts
A fascinating and extremely valuable collection of theories, tests, herbal formulas and special information pertaining to many facets of this dreaded disease. (65 pages)

Cookbook for Electro-Chemical Energies
The opening of this book describes basic principles of healthy eating along with some fascinating facts you may not have heard before. The rest of this book is loaded with delicious, healthy recipes. A great value. (106 pages)

God Helps Those Who Help Themselves
This work is a beautifully comprehensive description of the seven basic physical causes of disease. It is wholistic information as we need it now. A truly valuable volume. (196 pages)

Good Health Through Special Diets
This book shows detailed outlines of different diets for different needs. Dr. Reidlin, M.D. said, "The road to health goes through the kitchen not through the drug store," and that's what this book is all about. (90 pages)

Hanna's Workshop
A workbook that brings together all of the tools for applying Hanna's testing methods. Designed with 60 templates that enable immediate results.

How to Counteract Environmental Poisons
A wonderful collection of notes and information gleaned from many years of Hanna's teachings. This concise and valuable book discusses many toxic materials in our environment and shows you how to protect yourself from them. It also presents Hanna's insights on how to protect yourself, your family and your community from spiritual dangers. (53 pages)

Instant Herbal Locator
This is the herbal book for the do-it-yourself person. This book is an easy cross referenced guide listing complaints and the herbs that do the job. Very helpful to have on hand. (109 pages)

Instant Vitamin-Mineral Locator
A handy, comprehensive guide to the nutritive values of vitamins and minerals. Used to determine bodily deficiencies of these essential elements and combinations thereof, and what to do about these deficiencies. According to your symptoms, locate your vitamin and mineral needs. A very helpful guide. (55 pages)

New Dimensions in Healing Yourself
The consummate collection of Hanna's teachings. An unequated volume that compliments all of her other books as well as her years of teaching. (150 pages)

Old Time Remedies for Modern Ailments
A collection of natural remedies from Eastern and Western cultures. There are 20 fast cleansing methods and many ways to rebuild your health. A health classic. (105 pages)

Parasites: The Enemy Within
A compilation of years of Hanna's studies with parasites. A rare treasure and one of the efforts to expose the truths that face us every day. (62 pages)

The Pendulum, the Bible and Your Survival
A guide booklet for learning to use a pendulum. Explains various aspects of energies, vibrations and forces. (22 pages)

The Seven Spiritual Causes of Ill Health
This book beautifully reveals how our spiritual and emotional states have a profound effect on our physical well being. It addresses fascinating topics such as karma, gratitude, trauma, laughter as medicine . . . and so much more. A wonderful volume full of timeless treasures. (142 pages)

Spices to the Rescue
This is a great resource for how our culinary spices can enrich our health and offer first aid from our kitchen. Filled with insightful historical references. (64 pages)